a homework manual for biblical living

wayne a. mack

D0062426

vol. 1 personal and interpersonal problems

P U B L I S H I N G

P.O. BOX 817 • PHILLIPSBURG • NEW JERSEY 08865-0817

ISBN: 0-87552-356-0

CONTENTS

INTRODUCTION

In recent years it has been my privilege to lecture to church leaders in various parts of the United States on the subject of Biblical counseling. I have frequently told church leaders that God has given us in His Son, in His Spirit, and in His Word resources for helping people that no non-Christian counselor has. Consequently, I have suggested that we who are Christians should not run from the ministry of counseling but rather should welcome it and heartily engage in it.

After these lectures I have had many church leaders come to me and say, "I wholeheartedly agree with you and I am studying the Scriptures and other writings about Biblical counseling to become more competent to counsel. I believe I am improving and becoming more skillful in helping people with their problems, but there is one area where I find myself in need of much help. I know that the counseling session is not the 'magic hour' where the expert solves problems and changes people. I know that I must give people good Biblical homework that will hasten their improvement and help them to find their own solutions to problems. But that's my problem. I sometimes don't know what homework to give. Could you recommend a book that gives specific examples and samples of the kind of homework I might give to people with different kinds of problems?"

When asked this question, I have responded by saying that there are some samples of good homework in the various books written by Dr. Jay E. Adams and also in a marriage manual which I wrote, entitled, *Strengthening Your Marriage* (Presbyterian and Reformed Publishing Company). Many of these men have replied, "I know about these resources, but would like to have more. Please give some thought to producing a book that would provide more suggestions."

Well, this manual is an attempt to provide the "more" which has been requested. Included in this manual are homework assignments designed to help people overcome various personal or interpersonal problems. I have personally used this material with counselees and have seen God use it to help people to discover from His Word how to overcome many serious problems. I recognize that much work still needs to be done to improve these assignments and to develop homework that will be of assistance with problems not mentioned in this manual. Many of these assignments have been done and redone, and I'm still not satisfied. However, I have decided to send them forth with all their deficiencies to try to fill a void that exists for homework which is Biblical. I shall be deeply grateful if God uses this attempt to manifest His glory in the increased sanctification of His people.

In the future (D.V.) I hope to produce a homework manual which will supplement the material in *Strengthening Your Marriage* and to add other Biblical assignments to this manual.

Wayne A. Mack

ANGER

Help for Overcoming Sinful Anger, Bitterness, Resentment

Anger, like every other emotion, may be a good and useful emotion put to constructive, godly use (Mark 3:5; Ps. 7:11; Eph. 4:26). Or it may be a sinful emotion, which is used in ungodly, harmful, and destructive ways. This study is designed to help you discern between sinful and righteous anger and to aid you in overcoming the sinful expressions of anger which are harmful and destructive.

A. At whom or what is your anger most frequently directed?

    1. Other people _____

    2. Your circumstances or environment _____

    3. Yourself _____

    4. God _____

B. Describe the last three situations in which you became angry.

    1. _____

    _____

    2. _____

    _____

    3. _____

    _____

C. Discern and write down what the following verses have to say about the *wrong* way to handle anger. You are handling anger in a sinful and unbiblical manner when you:

    1. Ephesians 4:26, 27: Refuse to admit that you are angry. Clam up and pretend nothing is wrong. Make this way of dealing with anger a practice.

    2. Proverbs 17:14: Pick a fight as soon as you can. Be as nasty as you can.

    3. Proverbs 29:11, 20: _____

    _____

1

4. Matthew 5:21, 22: ______________________

5. Ephesians 4:31: ______________________

6. Proverbs 26:21: ______________________

7. Proverbs 15:1: ______________________

8. Colossians 3:8: ______________________

9. Romans 12:17, 19: ______________________

10. I Peter 3:9: ______________________

11. I Corinthians 13:5: ______________________

12. Philippians 4:8: ______________________

D. Discern and write down what the following verses have to say abou the *right* way to handle anger. Constantly review what God says about the right way of handling anger and deliberately seek to obey Him.

1. Romans 12:19-21: Never take your own revenge; turn the matter of punishment over to God; seek to help your enemy in specific ways.
2. Ephesians 4:26: Acknowledge that you are angry and seek to solve the problem immediately. Don't allow unresolved problems to pile up.
3. Ephesians 4:29: ______________________
4. Ephesians 4:32: ______________________
5. Matthew 5:43, 44: ______________________

6. Proverbs 19:11: _____

_____

7. Proverbs 15:1: _____

_____

8. Proverbs 15:28: _____

_____

9. Proverbs 16:32: _____

_____

10. Proverbs 25:28: _____

_____

11. Proverbs 14:29: _____

_____

12. Proverbs 29:11: _____

_____

13. Psalm 37:1-11: _____

_____

14. I Peter 3:9: _____

_____

15. Galatians 5:16-23: _____

_____

16. Romans 8:28, 29: _____

_____

17. Matthew 5:1-12; I Thessalonians 5:18: _____

_____

18. Ephesians 5:20: _____

_____

19. I Corinthians 10:13: _____

_____

20. Genesis 50:20: _____

_____

21. James 4:6: _____

_____

22. I Corinthians 6:19, 20: _____

_____

23. Matthew 18:21-35: _____

_____

E. Examine your own life in the light of Matthew 5:1-12; Galatians 5:22, 23; and II Peter 1:5-8 and list the qualities mentioned in these passages which are most lacking in your life. Ask a godly Christian for his evaluation. God wants to use all circumstances to develop these qualities in your life. Sinful anger overlooks this fact.

1. _____

2. _____

3. _____

4. _____

5. _____

6. _____

7. _____

8. _____

9. _____

10. _____

11. _____

12. _____

F. Consider how God may use your present irritations and annoyances to reveal your lack of these qualities and to develop them. When you are tempted to become sinfully angry, consider God's purpose for the trial.

G. Consider and write out some of the benefits that your problems or irritations may bring to you. Remember Romans 8:28; Job 23:10. God has a good purpose for everything that comes into the Christian's life.

1. Isaiah 43:1-3: Deeper communion and fellowship with God.

2. I Corinthians 11:31, 32: Stimulates self-examination.

3. Psalm 119:71: New insight into Scripture.

4. Romans 5:2-5: _____

5. II Corinthians 1:3-6: _____

_____

6. Hebrews 12:5-11: _____

7. II Corinthians 12:7-10: _____

_____

8. Matthew 5:10-12: _____

_____

9. I Peter 4:12-16: _____

_____

10. Psalm 119:67: _____

11. Psalm 50:15: _____

12. Philippians 3:10: _____

13. James 1:2-5: _____

14. I Peter 1:7: _____

H. Which of the following do you consider to be your "rights"? Usually we become sinfully angry because we think some "right" is being denied.

1. Right to have and control personal belongings _____

2. Right to privacy _____

3. Right to have and express personal opinions _____

4. Right to earn and use money _____

5. Right to plan your own schedule _____

6. Right to respect _____

7. Right to have and choose friends _____

8. Right to belong, be loved, be accepted _____

9. Right to be understood _____

10. Right to be supported _____

11. Right to make your own decisions _____

12. Right to determine your own future _____

13. Right to have good health _____

14. Right to date _____

15. Right to be married _____

16. Right to have children _____

17. Right to be considered worthwhile and important _____

18. Right to be protected and cared for _____

19. Right to be appreciated _____

20. Right to travel _____

21. Right to have the job you want _____

22. Right to a good education _____

23. Right to be a beautiful person _____

24. Right to be treated fairly _____

25. Right to be desired _____

26. Right to have fun _____

27. Right to raise children your way _____

28. Right to security and safety _____

29. Right to fufilled hopes and aspirations _____

30. Right to be successful _____

31. Right to have others obey you _____

32. Right to have your own way _____

33. Right to be free of difficulties and problems _____

34. Others _____

I. Which of the aforementioned "rights" are you being denied, and by whom?

Right	By Whom

1. Personal belongings

2. Privacy

3. _____

4. _____

5. _____

J. Consciously recognize that, if you are a Christian, you and all you have and are (your rights included) belong to God (I Cor. 6:19, 20; Rom. 12:1; Ps. 24:1). Acknowledge this and dedicate all that you are and have, including your "rights," to God. Trust Him to take care of His property. Cease to think in terms of your "rights" and concentrate on God's will and purpose and promises. For a while, until the fact that all your "rights" belong to God reaches the awareness level, you will want to specifically dedicate your "rights" to God on a regular basis.

K. The following is a recommended procedure you should follow if you desire to "put off" the sinful, destructive, unbiblical use of anger and "put on" the biblical, constructive use of anger. When something occurs which might lead to bitterness (clamming up, internalization of anger, resentment, hurt feelings, hostility, a grudge) or an explosion (angry words, verbal abuse, accusations, physical abuse, gossip, slander, retaliation of some sort, blaming, sarcasm, put downs, exaggeration, shouting), you should immediately put the following procedure into practice. You must do this *every time* you are tempted to become sinfully angry. Remember, "there is a way of escape" (I Cor. 10:13), "the fruit of the Spirit is . . . *self control*" (Gal. 5:22, 23), "God *has* . . . *given us* the Spirit of *power,* and *love* and of *self discipline*" (II Tim. 1:7). With promises like these from a God who cannot lie, there is no excuse for defeat, and there is every reason for victory. Here, then, is a procedure for victory. When a potentially distressing, fretful circumstance arises:

1. Immediately ask God to help you handle it in a God-honoring, Biblical way.

2. Remind yourself that God is sovereign. He could have prevented this circumstance from arising. He can now empower you to face it, and if you face it His way it will serve a positive, constructive purpose.

3. Thank God for the victory He is going to give you and the blessing He is going to bring into your life through this trial.

4. Consider what witness, service, modeling opportunities this situation may provide. Others are watching you, and you can now demonstrate the sufficiency of Christ, the reality and power of Christianity, the tremendous relevance and practicality of the Word of God in a fantastic way. Think of this and expect God to use you.

5. Examine yourself to see if you have done anything to promote the situation. Have you been lazy, irresponsible, stubborn, critical, wasteful, ungrateful, bossy, haughty, overly demanding, a nag, inconsiderate, unwilling to change or give in to other people, unmerciful, rude, crude, proud, too stern or austere, unfriendly, boastful, deceitful, sloppy, disorganized, jealous or envious, unmannerly, manipulative, suspicious, selfish, morose, solemn, sensi-

tive, negative and pessimistic? Often we sow the wind and reap the whirlwind. With what measure we dish it out we receive it back. Our problems are often the mirror of our own faults. According to the Bible, we roll a stone and it rolls back on us; we dig a pit and then fall into it ourselves; we are taken captive by our own iniquities.

6. Consider what character quality God may be trying to develop in you through this situation. If I am being unjustly accused, He may be trying to develop meekness or love or joy or patience or self-control or forgiveness, or poverty of spirit. My initial, natural response to the situation may pinpoint a deficiency and reveal what God wants to do in my life. I must acknowledge my deficiency and ask God to use circumstances to develop Christian traits to overcome these deficiencies.

7. Discern which "rights" of yours are being denied or neglected in this situation. Do you think you have a right to be respected, and is that why you are becoming upset because your wife won't fulfill your wishes? Do you think you have a right to be appreciated, and is that why you are becoming resentful toward someone who has criticized you or won't express his indebtedness to you? Identify what you think you are being denied and then turn the matter over to God. You belong to Him. He knows what you really need (Phil. 4:19). Trust Him to take care of you. He knows what things you have need of even before you ask (Matt. 6:25-34). Believe that God is much wiser than you. He knows much better than you what you really need, and He will supply what you need if you handle matters His way.

Turning your rights over to God doesn't mean you must become a doormat. It does not mean that you never make your desires known, or that you never oppose, rebuke, insist, exhort, or seek to correct a person. It does mean that you seek to do what you do in a Biblical, God-honoring fashion; for Biblical, God-honoring reasons; out of Biblical, God-honoring motives. It does mean that after you have done all that you may legitimately do, you leave the results with God and believe that He will bring to pass what is right and good for you. God's promise is that they who fear Him and seek Him shall not lack any good thing (Ps. 34:8-10). You must fulfill your Biblical responsibilities and then leave your "rights" to God. When He gives them back to you, consider them to be privileges and thank Him for them.

8. Seek to associate with those who are calm, self-controlled, handling problems God's way. You will learn from them, be strengthened and encouraged by them in the right way, and become like them (Prov. 13:20; II Tim. 2:22; Heb. 10:24, 25; Prov. 22:24, 25; 29:22; I Cor. 15:33; Heb. 3:12, 13; Prov. 27:17).

9. Discern specifically what God wants you to do and how He wants you to act at this time. Reflect on Biblical illustrations and exhortations that are applicable to your situation. Go over the passages mentioned under points C, D, E, and G of this study. Seek to obey these Biblical insights implicitly.

Anything less is disobedience (sin), and besides that anything less will not solve but compound the problem. The question is—How does God want you to handle the situation? Certain things you must not do. Certain things you must. Plan a Biblical cource of action. Do you need to confess your sin? (Compare K-5) Do you need to make restitution? Have you taken something that you never returned? Have you gossiped? Have you withheld something that you should have given? Should you agree to separate and give the matter some thought and prayer and then try to resolve the difficulty? What words would solve the problem rather than attack the other person or compound the situation (Eph. 4:29, 30)? Should you be willing to compromise or even give in to the other person? Have you tried to look at the situation from the other person's viewpoint? Have you tried to role play the situation, taking the other person's place? Have you put the best possible interpretation on what the other person has said or done? Do you allow things to build up or do you deal with one issue at a time? Do you need to seek the counsel of some Biblical counselor (your pastor, another godly Christian, or a professional Christian counselor) to help you discover God's way of handling the situation? How can you express kindness and concern for the person with whom you are having problems (Rom. 12:14-21)? As a Christian you must not attempt to overcome evil with evil, but with good. You must neither hold resentment under, nor give full vent to, your anger. Rather you must learn how to control your anger and use it for constructive purposes. You must release your anger under control. This can be done only if you allow your feelings to activate your words and actions and if you learn the habit of being guided by a mind that is controlled and marinated and instructed by solid Biblical principles. To make sure that this happens (to change the sinful habit patterns which have become deeply ingrained), it may be helpful for a time to actually write out how you should deal with tough situations, how you should respond, exactly what you should say. Check your plan out with someone who is wise in spiritual matters, and if this person agrees that yours is a Biblical course of action, put the plan into operation. Do this again and again until it becomes rather normal for you to handle situations in a Biblical fashion. This, of course, is work, but it's worth it. God wants you to live this way. Your relationships with others will improve. Your health may even improve. You'll be happier and your testimony for Christ will be much more powerful. This plan for overcoming sinful anger will work if you will put it to work.

In this study I want to include diagrams which depict what you have been studying about the wrong and right ways to handle anger. Hopefully these diagrams will fix in your mind the truths you've been studying. They are taken from a pamphlet by Dr. Jay Adams on "What to Do When Anger Gets the Upper Hand?"

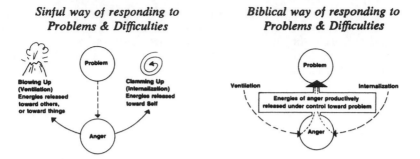

Sinful way of responding to Problems & Difficulties

Blowing Up (Ventilation) Energies released toward others, or toward things

Problem

Clamming Up (Internalization) Energies released toward Self

Anger

Biblical way of responding to Problems & Difficulties

Problem

Ventilation   Internalization

Energies of anger productively released under control toward problem

Anger

L. Habit patterns and responses that have been part of us for years are not always easy to change. In fact, the reverse is usually true. But, by the power of God, we can change. We can control our anger. We don't need to continue to explode or become bitter. Thus far we have seen that to change we must plan ahead, we must think Biblically, and exercise self-control when stress situations arise. In addition to these things, the person who wants to change should review what he is doing on a daily basis. Daily fill out the following chart, which will reveal your progress in changing sinful patterns. The chart was developed by Dr. John Broger.

Problem or Circumstance	Sounded Off	Took It and Ground My Teeth	Followed the Scripture (Identify It)
1.			
2.			
3.			
4.			
5.			
6.			
7.			
8.			
9.			
10.			
11.			
12.			

13. _____

14. _____

15. _____

16. _____

17. _____

18. _____

19. _____

20. _____

ANGER

Study Guide for Overcoming Irritability (Anger)
(Abbreviated Form)
You can be a nice person.—Philippians 4:5

The Greek word, ἐπιεικές, used in Philippians 4:5 means forbearing, large hearted, gentle, courteous, considerate, generous, lenient, moderate. In summary, it is describing a quality which is the opposite of irritability, rudeness, and abrasiveness; it is describing a quality that would make a person nice instead of nasty. It is saying that if you are a Christian, you can be a nice person.

1. With whom or what are you most likely to be irritable? What is there about your surroundings that irritates you? About yourself? About your friends, associates, family? When are you most likely to be irritable? How do you express irritability?

2. Identify the last three times you became irritated and analyze what happened and what you did. If you can't remember three instances from the past, examine several times when you are prone to be irritated in the present and future.

3. Examine the following items and underline the things that tend to irritate you: when you don't get your own way; when others don't do what you want them to do; when others make mistakes; when others are slow to understand, appreciate, or accept your point of view; when others don't give you the respect or attention you desire; when others disagree with you, or criticize or oppose or rebuke or correct you; when others fail or are inefficient; when others insist on having their own way; when others won't cooperate with you or yield to you; when others won't leave you alone; when others deny you your rights; when you don't get what you want; when others interfere with your plans; when others will not change as you want them to change; when you don't get the promotion or position or grades you desire; when others say "no" to you; when others ignore you or treat others better than they treat you. Ask your mate or a close friend to evaluate you in terms of these situations.

4. In the light of the previous assignments make a list of specific ways in which you need to change to become a more forbearing, nicer person.

5. Study the following passages and notice how the people described reacted in potentially irritating circumstances. How would you have reacted in these instances? Did they manifest forbearance or irritability?
Genesis 4:1-14; Genesis 13:5-13; Genesis 30:12; Genesis 45:1-15; I Kings 12:6-15; John 13:1-17; Luke 9:51-56; Matthew 15:21-28; Matthew 20:17-24 (esp. vs. 24); Matthew 18:23-35; John 13:21-30; John 21:15-19; Acts 11:1-18; Acts 13:50-52; Acts 7:54-60; Acts 16:19-34.

6. Study the following verses and note what you must do to overcome irritability: John 17:17; Acts 20:32; II Timothy 3:15-17; Colossians 1:9-11; Proverbs 16:32; Proverbs 29:11; I Timothy 4:7; Proverbs 19:11; Proverbs 27:12; Proverbs 28:28; Proverbs 19:19; James 1:2-5; Philippians 1:12-19; Proverbs 22:24, 25; Romans 8:28, 29; Romans 5:3-5; James 4:6; Ephesians 5:20; I Corinthians 10:13.

7. Focus on several ways in which you need to change to become a nicer person. Make these items a constant matter of prayer, refuse to excuse yourself when you fail, confess your sins daily, and discipline yourself to work daily on becoming a more forbearing person. If you are a Christian and do this consistently, you will become a nicer person and become a better testimony for Christ.

ANXIETY AND WORRY

Anxiety Homework

1. Have daily Bible reading and prayer. Keep a written record of what you do and get out of your devotions.
2. Go to bed at the same time every night. Before going to bed, seek to relax. If need be, take a warm bath, pray for God's blessing on sleep (Prov. 3:24; Ps. 4:8; 127:2). Confess your sins and commit your problems into God's hands; exercise to the point of perspiration (exercise and worry are normally contrary to each other). Use night notes if necessary. (Put a pad and pencil within your reach of the bed and write down vital thoughts so that you will then feel free to go to sleep.) Do not stimulate your mind immediately before bedtime. Think about God's goodness, promises, etc. Put on thoughts that relax; make sure you have a comfortable mattress; avoid stimulants of any kind; don't eat before you go to bed. Seek to get seven to eight hours of sleep every night. Keep a record of how many hours you sleep each night.
3. Make a daily practice of listing the things for which you are thankful. Give thanks for several items specifically every day. Meditate on these items when you are tempted to be anxious.
4. Memorize and practice Philippians 4:8. Make a list of profitable things you can think and do when tempted to anxiety. Put your "think and do" list into practice whenever you are tempted to be anxious or depressed. Continue to add to this list.
5. Keep a daily journal of times you are tempted to be anxious; record what you were doing at the time, what was happening, what you were thinking about, what you did, what you should have done.
6. Set aside a period of time every day when you will talk to a godly, fruitful Christian about anything that would be mutually beneficial to both of you (Eph. 4:29, 30).
7. Do at least two fun things this week.
8. Faithfully fulfill your responsibilities as a husband, father, mother, wife, employee, student, etc., regardless of how you feel. Focus on obedience to God, not feelings.
9. Read and carefully outline the pamphlets by Adams, *What to Do When Fear Overcomes You,* or *What to Do About Worry.* Review these notes on worry often.
10. Begin working on a life notebook. Include in it a record of your devotions; your personal prayer list and how and when God answered your prayers; a list of prayer promises; a brief daily diary of what happens to you and what God is doing in you and through you; your personal goals. In formulating these goals be realistic, specific, and practical. In the future you will need to pray, review, and endeavor by God's help to fulfill these goals.

Study Guide for Overcoming Anxiety
You can be peaceful.—Philippians 4:6-9

1. Study the following verses and then write down everything they indicate about anxiety or worry. (Remember that in the King James Version the words care and careful are often synonyms for worry.) Luke 10:38-42; Proverbs 28:1; Ezekiel 4:16, 17; Luke 8:14; Luke 21:34; Proverbs 15:15; Psalm 38:6; Genesis 45:3; I Samuel 28:20-23; II Thessalonians 1:7; Psalm 77:4, 8, 9.

2. If you did not do this when you studied the previously mentioned verses, go back over them and write down the effects of anxiety on the person who worries (e.g., the anxious person often becomes critical, a complainer, jealous, or envious, depressed, fearful, timid, insecure, etc.).

3. Study Philippians 4:6-9 and note God's threefold program for overcoming worry.

   a. Verse 6—To overcome worry God says I must *pray properly*. Note at least four or five facts about the kind of prayer that overcomes worry.

   b. Verse 8—I must *think properly*. Note the kind of things you must think about if you are to become a peaceful person. Make a specific list of what some of these things are for you. Consider Romans 12:2; I Peter 3:14, 15; and Matthew 6:25-32. Plan specific things you can do to make sure you think properly. How can you change your negative, pessimistic thinking to Biblical thinking?

   c. Verse 9—I must *live properly*. Consider Proverbs 28:1 and Proverbs 1:33 and notice how anxiety is often connected with wrong living. Notice also the effect of fulfilling your God-given responsibilities. For example, some people are worried about losing their jobs because they aren't fulfilling Colossians 3:22-24 or Ephesians 6:5-8. Some people are worried about finances because they aren't good stewards of their finances. Look over your life and note where you are not fulfilling your God-given responsibilities. Then plan to make changes and focus on doing what God wants you to do today.

4. Think back over the past two weeks and reflect on those times when you were tempted to be anxious. Write down what you were doing at the time, what was happening, where you were, what you were thinking about, whom you were with, what was the time of day, what you did, what you would have done according to Philippians 4:6-9.

5. If you want to overcome anxiety and become a peaceful person, go through the procedures described under assignment four above every time you are tempted to become anxious. Then discipline yourself to put God's threefold program (Phil. 4:6-9) for overcoming worry into practice, regardless of how you feel. If you are a Christian and do this consistently, you can and will overcome anxiety and become a peaceful person.

6. Write Philippians 4:6-9 out on a card and memorize it. Reflect on it and implement it regularly.

15

BLAMESHIFTING

How to Deal with Blameshifting

(This homework was primarily developed by Raymond Richards)

1. What does the Bible have to say about man's natural condition?

    a. Genesis 6:5: _____

    b. Ecclesiastes 7:20: _____

    c. Romans 3:10: _____

    d. Romans 3:23: _____

    e. I John 1:8, 10: _____

    Because of man's pride, who does he naturally think is right? (Prov. 21:2):

    _____

    Who is responsible for your sins? _____

2. Read Matthew 7:1-5.

    a. What does Jesus say you should not do? _____

    b. What does He say you should do? _____

    c. Who is the guiltier party—the accused or the accuser? How do you know?

    (Refer to verse 4) _____

Assignment 1: List 50 ways you have been failing God as husband/wife, mother/father, church member, Christian, employee, student, etc.

3. Read the following verses and write out how each shifted the blame to someone else.

    a. Genesis 3:12: _____

    b. Genesis 3:13: _____

    How did blameshifting affect the relationship between Adam and Eve? _____

    _____

    _____

In what way is blameshifting contrary to the definition of love in I Corinthians 13:5, "Love does not behave itself unseemly, does not keep a record of wrongs. . . ."? _____

_____

_____

c. Proverbs 19:3: _____

Are you blaming God for the results of your own foolishness?

_____

d. Genesis 39:7-20: _____

_____

Are you blaming someone else for your own sin? If so, whom are you blaming and what sin have you committed? _____

_____

e. Numbers 13:26–14:6: _____

_____

Are you blaming God for your lack of faith? For your unwillingness to accept and learn from providential changes and trials in your life? Have you been blaming someone else because things just don't go the way you want them to go?

_____

_____

f. I Samuel 15:1-23, particularly verses 15, 21
   1. What did God specifically command Saul to do (vs. 3)?

   _____

   2. What did Saul do (vs. 9)? _____

   _____

   3. Whom did he blame (vs. 15)? _____

g. If we seek to justify our actions and shift the blame to someone else, what will be the result (Job 9:20)? _____

_____

4. How does God want you to deal with your sins?

    a. Proverbs 9:20: _____

    b. Psalm 32:5: _____

    c. Psalm 51:4: _____

    d. I Samuel 3:15-18: _____

    e. II Samuel 12:13: _____

    f. Psalm 103:3: _____

    g. I John 1:9: _____

    h. Matthew 5:23, 24: _____

    _____

    i. James 5:16: _____

    j. Micah 7:9: _____

Assignment 2: After you have made your list of failures (Assignment 1), ask God's forgiveness. If they have hurt another person, ask that person's forgiveness. If you have sinned against a group of people, go to that group and confess your sins publicly. *Your confession should be as public as the offense.*

5. What should be your response when someone blames you?

    a. Romans 12:17a: _____

    b. Romans 12:19: _____

    c. Philippians 4:4: _____

    d. I Thessalonians 5:18: _____

    e. I Peter 2:15: _____

    f. I Peter 2:23: _____

    g. I Peter 3:9: _____

    h. Titus 2:7, 8: _____

    i. I Peter 3:11: _____

    j. Ephesians 4:29: _____

    k. Luke 6:29: _____

    l. Luke 6:35: _____

m. II Samuel 16:5-12: _____

Assignment 3: Write out at least ten ways you can respond Biblically to someone who accuses you or blames you. Keep in mind that you want to "bless" rather than condemn.

Example: "I know I have that problem, Mary. Do you have any suggestions that will help me change?"

"Thank you for telling me that, John. I know I haven't been as faithful in keeping the house clean as I ought to be. Starting right now I'll make the home cleaner and more comfortable for you."

"I'm not sure I understand. Would you explain it more clearly?"

_____

_____

_____

_____

_____

_____

_____

_____

_____

_____

_____

_____

_____

_____

_____

_____

_____

_____

6. The Bible says "pursue peace with all men" (I Pet. 3:11) and "overcome evil with good" (Rom. 12:21). Make a list of 25 things you do or say to pursue peace and overcome evil with good.

Example: "Instead of complaining and blaming God for moving us to this new area, I am going to extend myself to my neighbors and ask them in for supper."

"If Mary is having a hard time getting supper ready, I'll set the table when I get home."

"Since the pastor is having a hard time of putting his message together because of his busy schedule, I am going to ask if I can do his correspondence for him."

7. To overcome blameshifting, you must:
   a. Take full responsibility for your own sins (Mic. 7:9).
   b. Thank God and others for bringing your sins to your attention (I Thess. 5:18).
   c. Confess your sins to God and to others whom you have offended (I John 1:8; James 5:16).
   d. Allow God to deal with the sins of others (Col. 3:25; Nah. 1:2).
   e. Seek to change in the areas where you have sinned (Eph. 4:24).
   f. Commend, bless, express appreciation, pray for others (Luke 6:35).
   g. Maintain a blameless testimony by good works (I Pet. 2:15).
   h. Always seek to put the best construction on what others say or do (I Cor. 13:5).

For your further edification, study these verses to discover how David handled a situation when he was mistreated by the wicked.

1. Read Psalm 37:1-5.

   a. What was the circumstance of David's problem (vs. 1)?

   _____

   b. What two commands does God give in verse 3?

   _____

2. What does God say will be the inevitable fate of evildoers (vs. 2)?

   _____

   Rather than retaliating toward those who seek your harm, according to verses 3, 4, 5 what should you be focusing on?

   _____

3. What promises does God give to those who trust Him and fulfill their responsibilities?

   a. Verse 3: _____

   b. Verse 4: _____

    c. Verse 5: _____

    d. Verse 6: _____

4. Should the focus of your life be on insisting on your rights or on fulfilling your responsibilities while trusting on God? _____

_____

5. How does retaliation evidence a lack of trust in God (cf. vs. 6:1; I Pet. 2:23)?

_____

_____

6. Are you developing a pattern of blameshifting because there are areas of your life where you are being unfaithful, where you are not "dwelling in the land and doing good"? If so, what are they? _____

_____

7. When has God "brought forth your righteousness as the light. . ."?

_____

_____

8. Are you more concerned about what others are thinking of you, about maintaining an image before others than you are about trusting God to exalt you and silence the foolish accusations of others by your good works?

_____

CHECK-UP SESSION

Name(s) _____

Date _____

Between now and your check-up session, please do the following things:
1. Maintain regular Bible reading and prayer time.
2. Attend a Bible-preaching church regularly. Become involved not merely as a spectator, but as a participant. Ask your pastor how you may serve Christ in your church.
3. Review the homework assignments from your counseling sessions. Check up on yourself regularly to see where you are applying the principles you learned and where there is still a lot of room for growth. Write down areas where there has been progress and areas where you are not making much progress. Be prepared to share these with your counselor at the check-up session. Give some thought to what you can do to speed up your progress in areas where you are failing.
4. Seek to serve other people in specific, tangible ways. If you have not done so, make a list of ways you may serve other people and put that list into practice regularly. Keep a record of ways you help others and be prepared to share it with your counselor.
5. Fulfill your responsibilities in the various areas of your life—spiritual, church, home, marriage, children, parents, finances, personal, physical, school, community, work, etc. Do what you ought to do regardless of how you feel. Note on paper areas in which you are succeeding or failing. What keeps you from fulfilling your responsibilities? How will you change? Be prepared to share with your counselor.
6. Make a list of Scripture you will memorize. Write the Scripture on 3 x 5 cards and carry them with you. Go over these verses in your spare time (Ps. 119: 9, 11).
7. Write down any problems or questions that arise between now and your next sessions. Seek to find and implement a Biblical solution, but if you don't, be prepared to seek help from your counselor.
8. Get proper rest, relaxation, and recreation. Guard against watching too much TV or the wrong kind of TV. Watch your reading material. Don't read things that are suggestive or lead you into temptation. Plan some recreation regularly which will involve active mental or physical participation. Keep a record of what you do.

COMMUNICATION

How to Become an Effective Communicator
Assignment for Study Session 1

A worksheet designed to help you evaluate your present success as a communicator and to discover how to improve.

A. Consider what happens when people don't communicate effectively.
1. Issues remain unclarified (Prov. 18:17).
2. Wrong ideas are uncorrected.
3. Conflicts and misunderstandings are unresolved (Matt. 5:23-26).
4. Confusion and disorder occur (I Cor. 14:33, 40).
5. Wise decision making is thwarted (Prov. 18:13).
6. The development of deep unity and intimacy is hindered (Amos 3:3).
7. Interpersonal problems pile up and barriers become higher and wider.
8. Boredom and discontentment and frustration develop.
9. Temptation to look for someone more exciting occurs.
10. We don't really get to know each other.
11. We don't receive spiritual help from each other.

B. Consider the ways you may communicate.
1. Visually—wink, closed eyes, etc.
2. Verbally—harsh voice, soft voice, etc. (What you say or don't say and how you say it.)
3. By notes or letters.
4. By smiles or frowns (facial expressions).
5. With your body (hands, feet, etc.).
6. By your presence or absence.
7. By a touch, a pat, or a hug.
8. By helping.
9. By a gift.
10. By the use of your talents or gifts.
11. By willingness or unwillingness to share.
12. By listening or not listening.

C. Consider different levels of communication—how have you and can you communicate on these levels? Give at least one instance if you can of how you have communicated on each of these levels.

1. Cliché level: _____

2. Casual conversation: _____

3. Sharing information or facts: _____

4. Supportive or encouraging or motivating: _____

5. Planning or decision-making: _____

6. Sharing ideas, opinions, feelings, emotions, or judgments: _____

   _____

7. Corrective, instructive, reproving, or challenging: _____

   _____

8. Disagreements or controversial issues: _____

D. Consider what Matthew 5:22-25 and Matthew 18:15, 21-22 have to say about maintaining good communications and relationships. Also Matthew 7:1-5 and I Peter 3:8.

1. _____

2. _____

3. _____

4. _____

5. _____

6. _____

7. _____

8. _____

9. _____

10. _____

E. List the personal insights and challenges you have received from this study. Be personal and specific.

1. _____

2. _____

3. _____

4. _____

5. _____

6. _____

7. _____

8. _____

How to Become an Effective Communicator

Assignment for Study Session 2

A. Make a list of things that you can share with other people.

1. _____
2. _____
3. _____
4. _____
5. _____
6. _____
7. _____
8. _____
9. _____
10. _____

B. Practice communicating with someone every day. Keep a daily log of whom you communicate with, when you communicate, and what you communicated about. Also rate the effectiveness of your communication efforts—excellent, good, fair, poor.

		Whom	*When*	*What*	*Effectiveness*
Sunday	1.				
	2.				
	3.				
	4.				
Monday	1.				
	2.				

	Whom	When	What	Effectiveness
	3.			
	4.			
Tuesday	1.			
	2.			
	3.			
	4.			
Wednesday	1.			
	2.			
	3.			
	4.			
Thursday	1.			
	2.			
	3.			
	4.			
Friday	1.			
	2.			
	3.			
	4.			
Saturday	1.			
	2.			
	3.			
	4.			

C. Make a list of helps to good communication found in the following verses.

1. Ephesians 4:15, 25: _____

2. Ephesians 4:29: _____

3. Ephesians 4:26, 27: _____

4. Ephesians 4:32: _____

5. Ephesians 5:33: _____

6. Psalm 141:3: _____

7. Isaiah 8:10, 20: _____

8. Matthew 19:3, 4: _____

9. Isaiah 50:4: _____

10. Ecclesiastes 12:10: _____

11. Proverbs 12:25: _____

12. Proverbs 15:1: _____

13. Proverbs 15:2: _____

14. Proverbs 15:28: _____

15. Proverbs 16:23, 24: _____

16. Proverbs 17:14: _____

17. Proverbs 18:23: _____

18. Proverbs 20:5: _____

19. Proverbs 20:15: _____

20. Proverbs 25:9: _____

21. Proverbs 25:11, 12: _____

22. Proverbs 25:15: _____

23. Proverbs 29:11: _____

24. Proverbs 31:26: _____

25. Galatians 5:13: _____

26. Romans 13:7, 8: _____

27. Proverbs 5:18, 19: _____

28. I Peter 3:1-7: _____

D. List the personal insights and challenges you have received from this study. Be personal. Be specific.

1. _____

27

2. _____

3. _____

4. _____

5. _____

6. _____

7. _____

8. _____

9. _____

10. _____

How to Become an Effective Communicator
Assignment for Study Session 3

A. Make a list of the circuit jammers (hindrances to good communication) found in these verses.

1. Ephesians 4:25: _____

2. Ephesians 4:29: _____

3. Ephesians 4:31: _____

4. Colossians 3:8: _____

5. Colossians 3:9: _____

6. Proverbs 11:12: _____

7. Proverbs 11:13: _____

8. Proverbs 12:16: _____

9. Proverbs 12:18: _____

10. Proverbs 15:1: _____

11. Proverbs 15:5: _____

12. Proverbs 16:27: _____

13. Proverbs 17:9: _____

14. Proverbs 18:2: _____

15. Proverbs 18:6: _____

16. Proverbs 18:8: _____

17. Proverbs 18:13: _____

18. Proverbs 18:17: _____

19. Proverbs 18:23: _____

20. Proverbs 19:1: _____

21. Proverbs 19:5: _____

22. **Proverbs 20:19:** _____

23. **Proverbs 20:25:** _____

24. **Proverbs 25:24:** _____

25. **Proverbs 26:18, 19:** _____

26. **Proverbs 26:20, 21:** _____

27. **Proverbs 26:22:** _____

28. **Proverbs 28:2:** _____

29. **Proverbs 29:20:** _____

30. **Proverbs 29:21:** _____

B. Examine your effectiveness as a communicator.

   1. What circuit jammers need to be eliminated?

      a. _____

      b. _____

      c. _____

      d. _____

      e. _____

      f. _____

      g. _____

      h. _____

      i. _____

   2. What helps need to be added or strengthened?

      a. _____

      b. _____

      c. _____

      d. _____

      e. _____

      f. _____

      g. _____

h. _____

i. _____

3. Ask someone who knows you well what you can do to promote better communications.

a. _____

b. _____

c. _____

d. _____

C. List the personal insights and challenges you have received from this study. Be personal and specific.

1. _____

2. _____

3. _____

4. _____

5. _____

6. _____

7. _____

8. _____

9. _____

10. _____

How to Become an Effective Communicator
Assignment for Study Session 4

A. Keep a record of times when you expressed concern and appreciation for the ideas, desires, interests, feelings, and actions of other people this week (Phil. 1:3; Prov. 31:28, 29).

1. _____

2. _____

3. _____

4. _____

5. _____

6. _____

7. _____

8. _____

B. List several occasions when you have admitted to other people that you were wrong or asked for forgiveness. Describe the circumstances.

1. _____

2. _____

3. _____

4. _____

5. _____

6. _____

7. _____

C. Make a record of some people you have criticized, what you criticized them for. Keep a daily log. Also try to recall your criticism of the past week.

Who	*What*
1. _____	_____
2. _____	_____

3. _____

4. _____

5. _____

6. _____

7. _____

8. _____

9. _____

10. _____

D. Make a list of things you can do to help other people (Phil. 2:3, 4). Put the list into practice. Keep a daily log of what you do for other people.

Things you can do	*Things you have done*

1. _____

2. _____

3. _____

4. _____

5. _____

6. _____

7. _____

8. _____

9. _____

10. _____

E. Study Ephesians 4:25-32; Romans 12:4-16; Romans 14:1–15:3; James 1: 19, 20; Proverbs 15:1; Proverbs 18:13; Proverbs 29:11; I Corinthians 13: 4-8; and Amos 3:2. Note how VITAL these verses say good communications are. Write down the verses that correspond to the words in the following outline.

GOOD COMMUNICATIONS REQUIRE (VITAL):

1. V   a. Variety (compare section B from session 1)

   _____

   b. Vocal communications _____

2. I   a. Common Interests   _____

   b. Intelligence   _____

3. T   a. Truthfulness   _____

   b. Timing   _____

4. A   a. Atmosphere   _____

   b. Affection   _____

   c. Acceptance   _____

5. L   Listening   _____

   _____

   _____

F. List the personal insights and challenges you have received from this study. Be personal and specific.

   1. _____
   2. _____
   3. _____
   4. _____
   5. _____
   6. _____
   7. _____
   8. _____
   9. _____
   10. _____

Communications

Write down what the Bible says about critical, angry, abusive words. Write down how you frequently err in your speech.

Proverbs 10:12: _____

Proverbs 10:14: _____

Proverbs 10:17: _____

Proverbs 10:18: _____

Proverbs 10:19: _____

Proverbs 10:32: _____

Proverbs 11:9: _____

Proverbs 12:6: _____

Proverbs 12:16: _____

Proverbs 12:18: _____

Proverbs 13:3: _____

Proverbs 14:17: _____

Proverbs 14:29: _____

Proverbs 15:1: _____

Proverbs 15:4: _____

Proverbs 15:18: _____

Proverbs 15:28: _____

Proverbs 16:27-28: _____

Proverbs 16:32: _____

Proverbs 17:9: _____

Proverbs 17:14: _____

Proverbs 17:27-28: _____

Proverbs 18:6-8: _____

Proverbs 18:13, 17, 21: _____

Proverbs 18:27: _____

Proverbs 19:11: _____

Proverbs 19:19: _____

Proverbs 20:3: _____

Proverbs 21:23: _____

Proverbs 22:24-25: _____

Proverbs 24:28, 29: _____

Proverbs 25:8: _____

Proverbs 25:21-23: _____

Proverbs 25:28: _____

Proverbs 26:17: _____

Proverbs 28:25: _____

Proverbs 29:20: _____

Proverbs 29:11: _____

Proverbs 29:22: _____

Proverbs 30:33: _____

Ecclesiastes 5:3: _____

Ephesians 4:31-35: _____

James 1:19, 26: _____

Matthew 12:34-37: _____

Galatians 5:19-21, 22, 23, 15, 16: _____

Psalm 19:13, 14: _____

Philippians 4:8: _____

Communication Guidelines

These communication guidelines were provided by Pastor Timothy Keller.

Proverbs 18:21; 25:11; Job 19:2; James 3:8-10; I Peter 3:10; Ephesians 4:25-32

Think about the guidelines and study the supporting Scripture verses.

1. Be a ready *listener* and do not answer until the other person has finished talking (Prov. 18:13; James 1:19).
2. Be *slow to speak.* Think first. Don't be hasty in your words. Speak in such a way that the other person can understand and accept what you say (Prov. 15:23, 28; 29:20; James 1:19).
3. *Don't go to bed angry!* Each day clear the offenses of that day. Speak the truth but do it in love. Do not exaggerate. (Eph. 4:15, 25; Col. 3:8; Matt. 6:34).
4. *Do not use silence to frustrate the other person.* Explain why you are hesitant to talk at this time (Prov. 10:19; 15:28; 16:21, 23; 18:2; 20:15; Col. 4:6).
5. *Do not become involved in quarrels.* It is possible to disagree without quarreling (Prov. 17:14; 20:3; Rom. 13:13; Eph. 4:31).
6. *Do not respond in uncontrolled anger.* Use a soft and kind response and tone of voice (Prov. 14:29; 15:1; 25:15; 29:11; Eph. 4:26, 31).
7. *When you are in the wrong, admit it and ask for forgiveness* and ask how you can change (Prov. 12:15; 16:2; 20:6; 21:2; Matt. 5:23-25; Luke 17:3; James 5:16).
8. *When someone confesses to you, tell him you forgive him.* Be sure it is forgiven and not brought up to the person, to others, or to *yourself!* (Prov. 17:9; Eph. 4:32; Col. 3:13; I Pet. 4:8).
9. *Avoid nagging* (Prov. 10:19; 16:21, 23; 17:9; 18:6, 7; 21:19; 27:15).
10. *Do not blame or criticize the other person.* Instead, restore . . . encourage . . . edify (Rom. 14:13; Gal. 6:1; I Thess. 5:11).
11. *If someone verbally attacks, criticizes, or blames you, do not respond in the same manner* (Rom. 12:17, 21; I Pet. 2:23; 3:9).
12. *Try to understand the other person's opinion.* Make allowances for differences.
13. *Be concerned about the other person's interests* (Eph. 4:2; Phil. 2:4; 3:15, 16).

What you have just studied are Biblical directives for promoting good communication and good relationships with other people. To really put some teeth into your effort to become more Biblical in your communicating, you may wish to sign the following agreement to implement these guidelines.

(If husband and wife, both sign)

Name _____ Date _____

Name _____ Date _____

Communication Improvement Exercise

1. Communication exercise:
   a. Visualize an automobile in your mind. Each person jot down two adjectives to describe it as you visualize it. Do the same for a chair, a house, a father, a good time, love.
   b. Share your notes with someone else. How much do your mental images differ? (Do with mate if you have a mate.)
   c. What does this tell you about communication?
2. What attitudes or messages do the following sentences convey to you? Do they convey respect, appreciation, consideration, encouragement, affection, love or disdain, disrespect, rudeness, animosity, hostility, rejection? Try to imagine yourself hearing these sentences from someone else.
   "You don't really care."
   "I really need you."
   "Well, what do you have to complain about today?"
   "It sounds like you had a difficult day. Is there any way I can help you?"
   "You shouldn't feel that way!"
   "I'm really sorry that you feel that way. How can I help? I'll be glad to pray for you and do anything I can."
   "You never kiss me."
   "Do you know what, honey? I really love you and like to have you hold me and kiss me."
   "Well, what do you know? Miracles still happen. You're ready on time."
   "Hey, hon, I just wanted you to know that I really appreciated the way you hurried to be ready to go on time."
   "Honey, you're terrific, and getting better all the time."
   "You always forget what I ask you to do."
   "I like the way you smile. It really brightens my day."
   "We ought to have company more often. It's the only time we get good food around here."
   "That was a super meal. You are a fantastic cook."
   "How comes you could get home early tonight when you don't do it other nights?"
   "Boy, it's really great you got home early. I really miss you during the day."
3. Reflect on the 13 "Communication Guidelines" on the previous page and—
   a. List the items that you most need to work on changing.
   b. Write down two specific actions you can take to improve these items.
   c. Share these with your mate and ask for help in changing. Get other suggestions concerning how you can improve these items. If you do not have a mate, share with a close Christian friend.

DATA GATHERING

Counseling Assignment for Session One
(Building Hope and Gathering Data)

1. Work on your counseling assignment at least 30 minutes a day, every day, between now and your next session. Remember, 30 minutes is only 3½ hours out of 168. Becoming a better person is certainly worth that much time.
2. Read Ephesians 4:17-32 before working on your assignments on the first two days and Romans 12:14-21 before working on your homework on the last two days. Ask God to help you do His will in your homework and your entire life.
3. During your first study session read through this assignment sheet in its entirety.
4. During your first study session read/listen to a tape entitled: _____

_____.

Write down 10 to 15 principles, concepts, insights, challenges, or applications discussed in the material presented. Copy two or three Scripture verses used. Try to memorize at least one of them during the week. Evaluate your life in the light of the insights you listed. Note where you have failed and how you need to change.

5. When you have finished assignment 4, if you have time in study session 1, move on to begin to make a list of your respective sins and failures. If the previous assignment fills up all your time in session 1, begin and complete this list in the other three sessions. To make this list, examine every area of your life. Note where you are failing in these various matters: church attendance and participation, your spiritual life, Bible reading and prayer, witnessing, friendships, recreation, physical care, habits, social relations, attitudes, work habits, emotions, family relations, parenthood, marriage, sex, speech, use of time, money, manners, cleanliness, organization, rudeness, concern for other people, selfishness, laziness, cooperation, stubbornness, generosity, decision making, school, expressing appreciation, relations with parents, amusements, bitterness, resentment, etc. In making this list, don't be abstract and vague. Don't merely say, "I am not what I ought to be," or "I'm not very nice to people." Rather, be specific and say:
   a. "I make excuses for not attending the services of the church."
   b. "I become angry and abusive in my speech when my parents tell me to be in at a certain time, or when my fellow employees push their work off on me."
   c. "I spend money foolishly on automobiles or clothes." "I don't keep my

checkbook balanced and sometimes my check bounces."
- d. "I allow my bedroom to be sloppy. I seldom make my bed, hang up my clothes, or put my shoes out of sight."
- e. "I do not mow the yard or pull weeds or wash the car or brush my teeth as my parents want me to."
- f. "I speak in a nasty tone of voice when someone disagrees with me or asks me to help him."
- g. "I seldom tell my mother how much I appreciate her cooking. I act as if I deserve it."
- h. "I blame others or my circumstances for my moodiness."

When you have finished listing your sins, ask God to forgive you. If your sins have involved other people, ask them to forgive you for the way you have failed them.

6. Read one chapter of Proverbs every day. List at least five directions for Christian living found in each chapter. Note where you need to change. Begin reading with chapter ____.

7. Make a list of specific ways that you would like to change. To help you do this, answer the question, "If God were to work a miracle and change you, what are 10 things you would want Him to do for you?"

8. Keep a daily record of problems that arise in your life this week and what you do about them.

9. *Bring your completed homework with you to your next session.* Your counselor knows from experience that success in counseling depends on how well you complete and apply your homework in this and succeeding sessions. Biblical counseling works when you and the counselor work. Your counselor commits himself to work and pray with you as long as you will make your counseling homework and application a priority matter in your life. You will make progress and your life will be fuller very quickly if you will take your homework and its application to your life seriously.

Sample of a Personal Log List
(List of Failures)

As mentioned in the title, this list is only a sample "log list." Go over it and personalize it. Make your own list using this as a guideline. Be honest and objective. Spare no punches. Be sure to add things that you see wrong in your own life that are not mentioned on this list. Specifically confess your sins to God and those whom you have wronged. Seek God's help to change. Bring your list to counseling sessions.

Read Matthew 7:2-5; Romans 14:7-23; Ephesians 4:25-32; James 5:16; I John 1:7-9; Proverbs 28:13.

1. I don't pray as I should. My prayer life is very sporadic.
2. I don't read and study the Bible as I should. I often miss days.
3. I make excuses for not attending the services of the church.
4. I am bitter about something that is or has happened at the church or in the home or at work or in my neighborhoood. (Note what you are bitter about and

   with whom.) _____

   _____

5. I have gossiped about _____ (name the

   person) with _____ (name of person).

6. I make plans and decisions without seeking God's will through prayer and Bible study and godly counsel.
7. I have exaggerated the faults and mistakes of _____ when I should have overlooked them.
8. I excuse my faults and failures and often blame them on others.
9. I am selfish and not very willing to let others have their way.
10. I do not obey my parents.
11. I am disrespectful to _____.
12. I think too much about myself and my needs and too little about the needs and desires and feelings of others.
13. I expect _____ to serve me and cater to me.
14. I often become impatient when _____.
15. I often become irritable with _____.
16. I become angry when my rights to privacy, to do what I want to do, to make

my own decisions, to be considered worthwhile and important, to be protected and cared for, to have fun, etc., are denied.

17. I am too concerned about having a lot of money.

18. I am too concerned about what people think or say. (About what?) _____
_____

19. I am inconsistent in my _____.

20. I am not thankful to _____ for _____.

21. I often complain about _____.

22. I do not use my gifts and abilities to serve the Lord as I should.

23. I have no plans, goals, or purposes in life.

24. I am often unhappy about _____.

25. I allow my bedroom to be very sloppy. (How? In what ways are you sloppy?)
_____

26. I spend money foolishly. (How?) _____
_____

27. I don't pay my bills. (Which ones are overdue?) _____
_____

28. I have a tendency to do what I feel like doing instead of what I ought to do.
(Give several examples.) _____
_____

29. I am often confused about _____.

30. I make sarcastic remarks to or about _____.
(Give specific examples of your sarcasm.) _____
_____

31. I have a tendency to dwell upon my past mistakes or sins. (Note what past
mistakes you dwell on.) _____
_____

32. I have a tendency to dwell on the past mistakes and sins of _____
_____. (List what past mistakes you dwell on.)
_____

33. I am not fulfilling my responsibilities to _____.

42

(List what specific responsibilities you aren't fulfilling.) _____

_____

34. I read the wrong kind of literature. (List what.) _____
35. I don't like being told what to do.
36. I am jealous or envious of _____.
37. I yell or scream at _____. (When? About what?)

_____

38. I make excuses for my _____ (laziness, temper, wastefulness, etc.).
39. I blame _____ for my _____.
40. I act as if God doesn't care or exist.
41. I am very stingy. (With what—time? money? etc. With whom?) _____

_____

42. I watch too much TV. (How much do you watch? Do you watch wrong programs?) _____

_____

43. I don't have time to do what I should be doing. (What? Why?) _____

_____

44. I make fun of the mistakes and weaknesses of _____.
45. I don't treat other people very nicely. (Whom? In what ways? Examples!)

_____

46. I become upset when others correct or criticize me. (Examples.) _____

_____

47. I don't listen to other people very well. I talk about myself too much.
48. I don't control my _____. I interrupt, correct, argue.
49. I am very bossy with _____. I like to be in charge of _____.
50. I seldom witness to my neighbors or fellow employees or family about Christ. (How often do you witness? What opportunities have you blown?) _____

_____

51. I don't encourage other people and put their needs ahead of my own. I am selfish. (How? In what ways? When?) _____

_____

52. I run from problems or ignore problems or attack others when I have problems instead of facing them and seeking to solve them God's way. (What problems?)

_____

53. I am failing my Christian service responsibility. (Which ones?) _____

_____

54. I am very rigid and inflexible. (About what?) _____

_____

55. I often feel sorry for myself. Brood. Cry. Feel blue. Withdraw. Pout.

56. I hurt other people and don't ask forgiveness. (How? Who?) _____

_____

57. I expect too much of other people. (In what ways?) _____

_____

58. I do not develop my gifts and abilities. (Which ones?) _____

_____

59. I don't always tell the truth. I sometimes lie to get out of a jam, or get my own way, or to impress others. (Give examples of lies.) _____

_____

60. I do things that I don't want _____ to know about. (What?)

_____

61. I am uncooperative about _____.

62. I am uncooperative with _____.

63. I am inconsiderate of _____ opinions, feelings, desires.

64. When asked to do something I often:
    a. Say I'll do it, but don't.
    b. Say I'll do it, but resent being asked.
    c. Tell people I'll do it later.
    d. Ask why someone else can't do it.

e. Ask why it needs to be done.

f. Tell people I can't do it.

65. I make decisions on my own and refuse to listen to advice. I am too independent and reject counsel. I don't ask for advice.

66. I do a lot of daydreaming. (About whom or what? When? How much time?)

_____

67. I often think immoral, impure thoughts. (When? About whom or what?)

_____

68. I have taken things from other people that don't belong to me. (What?)

_____

69. I have damaged the reputation of _____ _____.

70. I worry about _____.

71. I do not really believe that God is able to help me change my attitude, my life, my reactions.

72. I do not really believe that God sovereignly controls all circumstances and people in my life for good.

73. I give up and am frustrated easily. I am a quitter. I don't stick to jobs or chores that are difficult. I have failed in many things. (How? In what?)

_____

Data Gathering (1)

_____Journal

_____Name

_____Date

Directions: For the next _____ week(s), keep a daily record
of all events, activities, or situations (good or bad) that resulted in _____
_____. Note the time of day it occurred, and what
you did as well as what happened. If there were people involved, note who they
were.

Day 1. _____ (Write down the specific day)

Time	Situation	Response	People

Day 2. _____

Time	Situation	Response	People

Day 3. _____

Time   *Situation*   *Response*   *People*

Day 4. _____

Time   *Situation*   *Response*   *People*

Day 5. _____

Time   *Situation*   *Response*   *People*

Day 6. _____

Time   *Situation*   *Response*   *People*

Day 7. _____

Time   *Situation*   *Response*   *People*

Data Gathering (2)

Finish the following sentences with two or three answers each.

1. I am _____
   _____
   _____

2. I like _____
   _____
   _____

3. I am happy _____
   _____
   _____

4. I am unhappy _____
   _____
   _____

5. God is _____
   _____
   _____

6. A happy home _____
   _____
   _____

7. I want _____
   _____
   _____

8. I dislike _____
   _____
   _____

9. When I sin _____

_____

_____

10. Jesus Christ is _____

_____

_____

11. I have _____

_____

_____

12. When someone criticizes me _____

_____

_____

13. When I don't get my own way _____

_____

_____

14. I resent _____

_____

_____

15. I feel guilty _____

_____

_____

16. I would like to change _____

_____

_____

17. The Bible _____

_____

_____

18. I pray _____

19. I belong _____

_____

_____

20. I become angry _____

_____

_____

21. My greatest failures are _____

_____

_____

22. My chief sins are _____

_____

_____

23. I can _____

_____

_____

24. I can't _____

_____

_____

Data Gathering (3)—Youth
Questions for Self-Evaluation and Improvement

1. List the three biggest problems you face in your life.

   a. _____

   b. _____

   c. _____

2. What are the biggest problems you face in your:

   a. Relationship with your parents? _____

   _____

   b. Relationship with your brothers and/or sisters? _____

   _____

   c. School life? _____

   _____

   d. Relationship with members of the opposite sex (dating, etc.)? _____

   _____

   e. Relationship with people of the same sex? _____

   _____

   f. Own personal spiritual, physical, or emotional life? _____

   _____

3. Are you appreciated and liked by others? What do others appreciate about you? What makes you likeable?

   a. _____   e. _____

   b. _____   f. _____

   c. _____   g. _____

   d. _____   h. _____

51

4. In your opinion what constitutes success? In other words, describe what makes a person worthwhile or successful?

a. _____ d. _____

b. _____ e. _____

c. _____ f. _____

How does your opinion of success compare to God's evaluation of success?

_____

_____

5. List your three biggest fears— a. _____
the things you dread most—the
worst things that could ever hap- b. _____
pen to you.
 c. _____

6. Describe how you decide between right and wrong; the basis or method you

use in deciding what to do, say, or think. _____

_____

_____

7. As far as you are concerned, who is Jesus Christ and what does He mean to

you and your life? _____

_____

_____

_____

Please indicate your age _____ and sex _____.

DATING

A Christian Perspective

Case Study No. 1

In many countries, dating as we know it is unknown. Imagine that a Christian from a country that does not practice dating is visiting you. He soon observes the American dating process and is mystified. He comes to you and asks you, "Why do Christian young people in America date? What are the benefits of dating? What goals do Christian young people have for dating?" How would you answer him? (Matt. 6:33; Col. 3:17; Prov. 27:17; II Tim. 2:22; Heb. 10:24, 25).

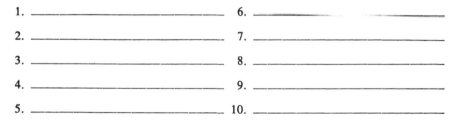

1. _____   6. _____

2. _____   7. _____

3. _____   8. _____

4. _____   9. _____

5. _____   10. _____

Case Study No. 2

A new Christian who knows very little about the Bible comes to you and says, "I need help. I realize that a Christian's life is to be governed in every respect by the Word of God. I want that, but I don't know that much about the Bible. I want to ask a girl out for a date, but I want my dates to be governed by the Word of God. Could you give me some help in answering two questions?"

1. "Whom should I date? Should I date just anybody who is available? Or does the Bible give some guidelines concerning the kind of people that we should date?" (Consider guidelines for selecting dates suggested by the following verses.)

   a. Proverbs 1:10-15: _____

   b. Proverbs 6:23: _____

   c. I Corinthians 15:33: _____

   d. II Corinthians 6:14-21: _____

2. "What should I do on a date and where can I go?"
   Answer in a general fashion by making a list of principles suggested by the following verses.

   a. Colossians 3:17, 23: _____

   b. Romans 13:13, 14: _____

c. Galatians 6:6, 7: _____

d. Romans 14:13: _____

e. I Timothy 4:12: _____

Now become more specific and list things a Christian could do or places a Christian could go on a date.

List Biblical guidelines for choosing a date. (Study the verses mentioned under No. 1 above.)

a. _____

b. _____

c. _____

d. _____

e. _____

f. _____

g. _____

List guidelines about what to do on a date.

1. General principles deduced from Scriptures listed under No. 2 above.

a. _____

b. _____

c. _____

d. _____

e. _____

f. _____

g. _____

2. Specific suggestions about wholesome, Christ-honoring dating activities.

Spectator Activities: *Participant Activities:*

a. _____   a. _____

b. _____   b. _____

c. _____   c. _____

d. _____   d. _____

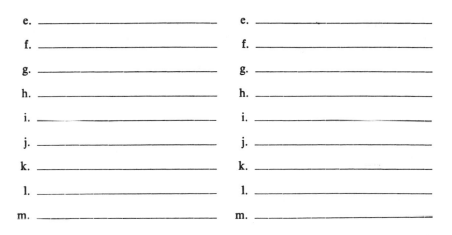

e. _____ e. _____

f. _____ f. _____

g. _____ g. _____

h. _____ h. _____

i. _____ i. _____

j. _____ j. _____

k. _____ k. _____

l. _____ l. _____

m. _____ m. _____

Case Study No. 3

Imagine that you are a youth director or pastor. A family in your church asks for an appointment because they are having some family problems. When they come for counseling, one of the first questions the teenage daughter asks is, "How old do you have to be before you can start to date?" What counsel would you give them?

1. _____

2. _____

3. _____

4. _____

Case Study No. 4

John is a young man who would like to date. He looks around and sees that all the Christian girls he knows are already going around with Christian fellows. What advice would you give him about getting a date? (Consider Prov. 3:5, 6; Matt. 7:7-9; Phil. 4:19.)

1. _____

2. _____

3. _____

4. _____

Case Study No. 5

Mary is a girl who wants to date; other girls in her church are being asked out, but no one asks her for a date. What counsel would you give her? What is it that causes some fellows and girls to be highly desirable, and what is it that causes others to strike out? What makes a person a successful dater? (Consider Mark 8:34, 35; Gal. 5:22, 23; I Cor. 13:4-8.)

1. _____

2. _____

3. _____

4. _____

5. _____

6. _____

Case Study No. 6

Tom is a handsome fellow. When he asks a girl out for a date, she usually accepts for the first date. But when she has dated him once, she makes excuses and refuses to go out with him again. What counsel would you give to him? (Consider I Cor. 13; Gal. 5:22, 23.)

1. _____

2. _____

3. _____

4. _____

Case Study No. 7

Jane is a girl who has been dating for about six months. To this point she has dated casually with several fellows, but two of the fellows and several of her girl-friends are pressuring her to make a choice among the fellows she is dating and settle down to go steady with one of them. Jane doesn't know if she should. She comes to you for advice. What would you tell her? What are the pros and cons of dating just one person? What are the advantages and disadvantages of going steady?

Advantages of going steady:

1. _____

2. _____

3. _____

4. _____

5. _____

6. _____

7. _____

Disadvantages of going steady:

1. _____

2. _____

3. _____

4. _____

5. _____

6. _____

7. _____

DEPRESSION HOMEWORK

1. Ask other people to pray for you and to provoke you to biblical obedience. Stay away from people who give you the wrong kind of sympathy and encourage your self-pity, excuse making, brooding, or the neglect of responsibilities. (Study I Cor. 15:33; Prov. 22:24, 25; 14:7; Gal. 6:1; Heb. 3:12, 13; 10:24, 25 concerning the kind of companions you need.) Decide whom you will ask for prayer and encouragement, and ask them.

2. Make a "think and do" list of profitable things you can think about and do when you are tempted to be despondent. Compare Philippians 4:8, 9. One of the first items on your "think and do" list might be to think about profitable things you can think about and do when you are tempted to be despondent. Keep this list with you on 3x5 cards, pull it out and get busy doing the things listed on it when you begin to feel blue.

3. Make a list of your responsibilities. Note which ones you are fulfilling well and regularly. *Also note* those that you have been or are prone to neglect because you don't feel like doing them. Ask God to help you do what you should do regardless of how you feel; plan a schedule which gives you time to do all that you really must do, and then get busy fulfilling your responsibilities. Don't focus on how bad you feel or how you dislike the task. Focus rather on God, His will for you, His promises and provisions for you, and the help He will give you to do anything that He wants you to do (Phil. 2:12, 13; 4:13). In all you do in obedience to God, count on His presence and help and blessing.

4. Make a list of at least 50 to 75 blessings that God has bestowed upon you. Look at every area of your life: spiritual, physical, family, financial, social, work, possessions, environment, community, housing, abilities, opportunities, etc. Continue daily to add to this list as you become aware of new benefits God is bestowing upon you. Remember Psalm 68:19 says He daily loads us with benefits. The blessings are there. We need to develop the habit of seeing and recognizing them. As you make your list of benefits, specifically thank God for each of them. Make it a daily practice to give specific thanks for particular things (Phil. 4:8; Ps. 34:1; Eph. 5:20).

5. Maintain a regular practice of daily Bible reading and study, prayer and meditation. Plan your procedure; schedule a regular time for your devotions; and put your plans into action. Keep a written record of what you get out of your devotional time. Ask mature Christians for help in making them more profitable. Seek immediately to implement what you learn and to share it with other people.

Study Guide for Overcoming Depression

You can be joyful.—Philippians 4:4

1. Study the following verses and list the things that could be circumstantial causes for depression.

   a. Psalm 32:3, 4: _____

   b. Psalm 73:1-14: _____

   c. Genesis 4:6, 7: _____

   d. Deuteronomy 1:28, 29: _____

   e. Psalm 55:2-8: _____

   f. Luke 24:17-21: _____

   g. II Samuel 18:33: _____

   h. I Samuel 1:7, 8: _____

   i. Habakkuk 1:1-4: _____

   Note particularly the circumstances that are present when you are prone to become depressed.

2. According to I Peter 1:3-5, II Corinthians 6:10, and I Thessalonians 4:13, are sorrow and rejoicing incompatible? Is there a difference between sorrow and depression?

3. Philippians 4:4 tells us to "rejoice in the Lord." What do the words "in the Lord" suggest about the way to overcome depression? What does it mean to be "in the Lord"? What does it mean to "rejoice in the Lord"? Are you "in the Lord"? List the reasons that you have for rejoicing "in the Lord."

4. Philippians 4:4 is a command, suggesting that being a joyful person and overcoming depression will require personal effort and responsibility. It will not happen automatically. It will happen *as you think and do* what God wants you to think and do. Study the following verses and note what you must do to overcome depression.

   a. Psalm 16:8, 9: _____

   b. Psalm 1:1-3: _____

   c. Psalm 32:1, 2: _____

58

d. John 13:17: _____

e. James 1:22-25: _____

f. Galatians 5:22, 24: _____

g. Romans 15:13: _____

h. Acts 13:52: _ _____

i. Proverbs 15:23: _____

j. I Thessalonians 2:19, 20: _____

5. Make a "think and do" list of profitable things you can think about and do when you are tempted to be despondent. Compare Philippians 4:8, 9. One of the first items on your think and do list might be to think about profitable things you can think about and do when you are tempted to be despondent. Keep this list with you on 3x5 cards, pull it out and get busy doing the things listed on it when you begin to feel blue.

6. Make a list of your responsibilities. Note which ones you are fulfilling well and regularly. *Also note* those that you have been or are prone to neglect because you don't feel like doing them. Ask God to help you do what you should do regardless of how you feel, plan a schedule which gives you time to do all that you really must do, and then get busy fulfilling your responsibilities. Don't focus on how bad you feel or how you dislike the task. Focus rather on God, His will for you, His promises and provisions for you, and the help He will give you to do anything that He wants you to do (Phil. 2:12, 13; 4:13). In all you do in obedience to God, count on his presence and help and blessing.

7. Focus on serving God and others in practical ways. Make a list of your abilities and gifts. Ask others to evaluate your strengths. Read Romans 12 and see where you fit into the picture. Make a list of specific ways in which you can serve God and other people. Begin immediately to put that list into practice. Keep a record for a little while of how you serve God and others. Plan how you will serve God in your home, church, community, school, job, etc.

True Happiness
(Overcoming Depression)

Study the following verses and note everything they have to say about happiness or blessedness. Write down what they have to say about what the blessed man does and how he is described; what God does for and says will happen to this person; note how you need to change to become a blessed, happy person. Evaluate how you measure up to the descriptions of the blessed man. Note where you are failing to be and do the things that God says bring blessedness. *Plan how and when you will change, and keep a record of the specific ways you will seek to implement Biblical principles.*

Psalm 1:1-6: _____

Psalm 2:12: _____

Psalm 32:1-6: _____

Psalm 40:1-4: _____

Psalm 41:1-3: _____

Psalm 84:4-12: _____

Psalm 106:3: _____

Psalm 128:1-6: _____

Psalm 112:1-9: _____

Psalm 119:1-7: _____

Psalm 127:3-5: _____

Psalm 144:15: _____

Matthew 5:1-12: _____

Luke 11:28: _____

John 13:17: _____

James 1:12, 21-25: _____

Philippians 4:1, 4: _____

Deuteronomy 12:18: _____

I Samuel 2:1-10: _____

I Chronicles 16:29: _____

Nehemiah 8:10: _____

Psalm 4:7, 8: _____

Psalm 5:11: _____

Psalm 13:5; 9:14: _____

Psalm 16:5-11: _____

Psalm 19:8: _____

Proverbs 19:23: _____

Jeremiah 15:16: _____

Luke 24:52: _____

John 15:1-12: _____

Galatians 5:22, 23: _____

I Thessalonians 1:6: _____

II Corinthians 1:12, 24: _____

II Corinthians 12:8-10: _____

Psalm 3:5, 6: _____

Ecclesiastes 5:12: _____

Psalm 127:2: _____

Proverbs 3:24: _____

I Thessalonians 5:11: _____

I Timothy 4:12, 18: _____

Philippians 4:12, 18: _____

I Corinthians 9:24-27: _____

II Timothy 2:5: _____

I Thessalonians 5:16-22: _____

Having done the above study, go back over the Bible verses and put the appropriate verses under the following headings. To experience true blessedness the Bible says you must:

1. Personally know the salvation which is in Jesus Christ: _____

2. Meditate regularly on God's Word, the Bible: _____

3. Fulfill your God-given responsibilities: _____

4. Confess and forsake your sins: _____

5. Faithfully spend time in prayer to God: _____

6. Praise and thank God in every situation: _____

7. Practice the presence of God by disciplining yourself to see all of life and every circumstance from a God-centered point of view: _____

8. Conscientiously serve God and people: _____

9. Use the gifts, abilities, and resources God has given you to help people: _____

10. Practical Biblical thinking and living in every situation: _____

11. Replace every pessimistic, defeatist thought with a Biblical thought: _____

12. Regularly seek fellowship with God's people: _____

13. Focus on becoming more like Jesus Christ in your character and attitudes:

14. Take care of yourself physically (sleep, exercise, diet): _____

15. Enjoy the variety of good things God has provided: _____

DEVOTIONS

How to Have a Quiet Time

Developed by Pastor Timothy Keller.

What is a "Quiet Time"?

A "Quiet Time" is a time of direct contact between your mind and God's, using the Bible and prayer. It is a time of dedication, cleansing, instruction, strengthening, and delight.

Bible study and prayer are not simply for our sake. God deeply desires our fellowship and worship—it gives Him joy and pleasure! (John 4:23). (Read *My Heart Christ's Home.*) Think from this perspective. If you're not moved by this fact, you have not understood it.

Communication with God must be daily (Josh. 1:8, 9). To know God (not just to know about God) is the goal. How we pray, delight, and think on God is the only true measure of whether our relationship with Him is alive (John 15:4). God bought (in blood) personal access to His presence for us. Even Abraham and Moses did not have this (II Cor. 3:12-18; Matt. 27:51). Moses was denied (Ex. 33:18, 20; II Cor. 4:6) that which we may have each morning (John 4:21-23).

The maintaining of a daily Q.T. is perhaps the most consistently difficult duty of the Christian life. Its difficulty is a humbling reminder of our lack of commitment to Him. It is an unalterable principle, however, that a Q.T. is necessary for Christian growth and obedience.

What are the goals of a Quiet Time?

First, *worship:* to get to know Him, to be humbled by His holiness, comforted by His love, strengthened by His presence.

Second, *change:* to root out sins and establish biblical attitudes and actions in your life.

How do I have a Quiet Time?

1. First, *meet God.* Still your heart, ask for His presence, concentrate. You may wish to praise Him a bit with a psalm to "warm up" your heart. Take a psalm and look for things to praise Him for.
2. Secondly, *listen to God* by reading a passage from His Word. Don't choose more than a chapter! Read it carefully, reverently, intelligently; read it more than once. Pick out what you think is the central thought of the passage. Record that thought and/or some other truth that has struck you, in your own words. Then determine what God's message is for you. Is there

63

a. A promise to claim?
b. A sin to confess?
c. A command to obey?
d. An example to follow?
e. An error to avoid?
f. A new thought about God?

Once this is determined, record it, and think of some way to practice or act upon the message if possible.

3. Thirdly, *talk to God through prayer*. The elements of prayer are—

a. Praise and thanksgiving. Be specific. Search your life and mind for things to thank Him for and then praise Him for. ("Thank you for letting me lose that contest! I see how wise you are—it would have been bad for me! Thank you for forgiving me after the way I acted yesterday; how merciful you are!")

b. Requests for self and others. Be specific. Unload your burdens and pour out your feelings. Also make a list of things to pray about for family and friends. Use the list daily to pray.

c. Confession. Search your life for sins committed since yesterday. Search for good deeds you avoided doing as well! Ask for cleansing, and then thank Him for his full forgiveness through Christ's blood.

How can I get started?

Make a contract right now to begin a daily Q.T. Be consistent in time and place. Start with about 20 minutes. It should be unhurried. The place for it should be quiet. Morning is ideal.

Use a notebook and/or a "Quiet Time Sheet." Expect dry periods! That's no excuse for stopping. Change your format, or the book of the Bible you are reading, every so often to avoid stagnation.

Share what you are learning in your Q.T. with other Christians. Get hold of a good Q.T. guide, if you wish. The pastor will be able to show you a variety of materials.

Quiet Time Sheet
(See "How to Have a Quiet Time")

Date _12/22/15._

1. *Meet God*

2. *Listen to God*   Passage read ___Col 3___

   a. Best things I noticed today.

   Reference: _____

   The thought in my own words:
   central thought :

   b. How it applies to me.

   Reference: _____

   The truth to apply:

   My plan:

3. *Talk to God*

   Confession   Requests for self and others   **Praise and thanksgiving**

Quiet Time Sheet
(See "How to Have a Quiet Time")

Date _____

1. *Meet God*

2. *Listen to God*   Passage read _____

   a. Best things I noticed today.

   Reference: _____

   The thought in my own words:

   b. How it applies to me.

   Reference: _____

   The truth to apply:

   My plan:

3. *Talk to God*

   Confession   Requests for self and others   Praise and thanksgiving

Quiet Time Sheet
(See "How to Have a Quiet Time")

Date _____

1. *Meet God*

2. *Listen to God*   Passage read _____

   a. Best things I noticed today.

   Reference: _____

   The thought in my own words:

   b. How it applies to me.

   Reference: _____

   The truth to apply:

   My plan:

3. *Talk to God*

   Confession   Requests for self and others   Praise and thanksgiving

Quiet Time Sheet
(See "How to Have a Quiet Time")

Date _____

1. *Meet God*

2. *Listen to God*   Passage read _____

   a. Best things I noticed today.

   Reference: _____

   The thought in my own words:

   b. How it applies to me.

   Reference: _____

   The truth to apply:

   My plan:

3. *Talk to God*

   Confession   Requests for self and others   Praise and thanksgiving

Simple Inductive Method
A B C Method

For the next week study the book of _____, using the following procedure. Study a chapter a day. Bring a written record of your devotions to the next counseling session.

First, *PRAY*

Ask God to teach you and to make His truth clear and vital to you.

Second, *READ*

Go through the passage several times. Jot down things that puzzle you. Also record cross references to other Bible passages that come to mind.

Third, *STUDY*

ANALYZE

1. List the basic facts. What is it saying about what subjects? What is happening, when, where, why, involving whom?
2. Give the passage a title.
3. Outline it (break it into divisions or sections), and then summarize each section in your own words.[1]
4. Summarize the theme or main point of the whole passage in a sentence.

BEST VERSE

1. Choose the verse that convicts you, inspires you, or enlightens you the most.
2. Meditate on it.
   a. Think of the special importance of each word.
   b. Look at it from different angles.

CONTRACT

1. Apply the teaching by asking:
   a. Is there a new thought about God?
   b. A promise to claim?
   c. A command to obey and a result to see?
   d. A sin to confess?
   e. A pattern to follow?
2. Then ask:
   a. Where did I last miss this? Where can I next practice this?
   b. Why is God telling me this now?
3. Then write out a specific plan for obeying the truth. As much as possible list the time, place, etc. When finished doing this, refer to reference works for answers to questions that puzzle you. Look up cross references.

Once a week choose your best verse of the week and memorize it!

---

1. Each section can be outlined and broken into subsections in turn, then each subsection can be outlined as well! Use the ABC method in whatever degree of detail you desire.

Growth Time Sheets

Pray for understanding.—Psalm 119:18; Ephesians 1:17

PASSAGE .... DATE .... NAME ....

Observation	Interpretation	Application	Transmission	Examination
What does the passage say? Write out the text.	What does the passage mean? Write out what you think the passage means.	What does this passage mean in your life? What *specific* changes do you need to make? Write down what you are going to do with whom or for whom and when you will do it.	With whom will you share your discoveries? Pray about it and do it now.	What happened in your life because you applied this truth? What changes took place?

Self-Confrontation Bible Study

For meaningful devotions, try S M A C

SCRIPTURE
READING TODAY: .... Developed by Dr. John Broger.

VSS.	What does the Bible SAY?	What does it MEAN?	For me, how does it APPLY	What will I do to CHANGE

Evaluate **CHANGE**
Weekly

FEAR

Study the following verses and note everything they have to say about fear. Write down what they have to say about the results of fear, the causes of fear, and the solution to fear. Specifically write down what causes your fear, what the results of your fear are, and a Biblical strategy for overcoming sinful fear. To discover the causes of your fear, keep a daily journal of the times you are most fearful: note exactly when it happens, where you are, what happened, with whom you are, what you think about, and what you do when you are tempted to be fearful. Evaluate your response in light of what Scripture indicates you should do. Did you handle Biblically the temptation to fear? If not, how did you fail? How, specifically, should you change your response when tempted to become fearful?

1. Note the results of fear.

Luke 21:26: _____   Genesis 21:16, 17: _____

_____   _____

Proverbs 29:25: _____   Genesis 26:6, 7: _____

_____   _____

I John 4:18, 19: _____   I Samuel 15:20-25: _____

_____   _____

Proverbs 10:24: _____   Galatians 2:12: _____

_____   _____

Proverbs 28:1: _____   Mark 4:35-41: _____

_____   _____

Matthew 25:14-25: _____   Numbers 14:1-4: _____

_____   _____

Deuteronomy 28:58-67: _____   Matthew 26:69-74: _____

_____   _____

Leviticus 26:27-37: _____   _____

_____   _____

2. Write down the causes of fear.

I John 4:18, 19: _____   Genesis 21:16, 17: _____

_____   _____

Proverbs 28:1: _____   Genesis 26:6, 7: _____

_____   _____

Proverbs 1:33: _____   Matthew 10:28: _____

_____   _____

Proverbs 29:25: _____   Galatians 2:12: _____

_____   _____

Hebrews 13:5, 6: _____   Psalm 23:4: _____

_____   _____

John 7:13; 20:19: _____   Psalm 56:4: _____

_____   _____

Hebrews 2:15: _____   Matthew 26:69-74: _____

_____   _____

Ezekiel 11:8: _____   Mark 4:35-41: _____

_____   _____

Genesis 32:11 _____   Numbers 13:25–14:5: _____

_____   _____

Psalm 46:2, 3: _____   _____

_____   _____

3. Write down the solution to fear.

I John 4:18, 19: _____   II Timothy 1:7: _____

_____   _____

Psalm 112:1, 7, 8: _____   Proverbs 3:21-24: _____

_____   _____

Hebrews 13:5, 6: _____   Genesis 32:7-12: _____

_____   _____

Psalm 27:1-3: _____

_____

Proverbs 14:26, 27: _____

_____

Psalm 34:4: _____

_____

Psalm 46:1-10: _____

_____

I Peter 3:13-15: _____

_____

II Timothy 1:7: _____

_____

Genesis 32:7-12: _____

_____

Psalm 55:5-8: _____

_____

Proverbs 10:27: _____

_____

Proverbs 1:33: _____

_____

Psalm 34:4: _____

_____

Psalm 23:4: _____

_____

Joshua 1:9: _____

_____

Psalm 111:10: _____

_____

Proverbs 22:4: _____

_____

Hebrews 13:5, 6: _____

_____

II Chronicles 20:1-3: _____

_____

_____

FINANCES

You and Money

A. What truths do the following passages suggest about the attitudes we should have toward the acquisition and use of money?

1. Deuteronomy 8:17, 18: _____

   _____

2. I Chronicles 29:11, 12: _____

   _____

3. Ecclesiastes 5:19: _____

   _____

4. Ecclesiastes 5:10: _____

   _____

5. I Timothy 6:6-10: _____

   _____

6. I Timothy 6:17-19: _____

   _____

7. Luke 12:13-21: _____

   _____

8. Hebrews 13:5: _____

   _____

9. Philippians 4:11-19: _____

   _____

10. Proverbs 12:10: _____

   _____

11. Proverbs 11:28: _____

_____

12. Proverbs 11:24, 25: _____

_____

13. Proverbs 13:11; 14:23: _____

_____

14. Proverbs 13:18: _____

_____

15. Proverbs 15:6: _____

_____

16. Proverbs 15:16, 17: _____

_____

17. Proverbs 15:27: _____

_____

18. Proverbs 16:8: _____

_____

19. Proverbs 16:16: _____

_____

20. Proverbs 20:4: _____

_____

21. Proverbs 21:5, 6: _____

_____

22. Proverbs 21:25, 26: _____

_____

23. Proverbs 22:1, 4: _____

_____

24. Proverbs 23:1-5: _____

_____

25. Proverbs 24:30-34: _____

_____

26. Proverbs 27:24: _____

_____

27. Proverbs 28:6: _____

_____

28. Matthew 6:19, 20: _____

_____

29. Luke 6:27-38: _____

_____

30. Ephesians 4:28: _____

_____

31. II Thessalonians 3:7-12: _____

_____

32. Romans 13:6, 7: _____

_____

33. Matthew 17:24-27: _____

_____

34. Matthew 22:15-22: _____

_____

35. Proverbs 22:7: _____

_____

36. Matthew 15:1-6: _____

_____

37. II Corinthians 12:14: _____

_____

38. I Timothy 5:8: _____

_____

39. Acts 20:35: _____

_____

40. Matthew 16:26: _____

_____

41. Galatians 6:6; I Corinthians 9:11, 14: _____

_____

42. II Corinthians 9:6-12: List several principles of giving found in these verses.

a. _____

b. _____

c. _____

d. _____

e. _____

f. _____

43. Deuteronomy 15:10, 11: _____

44. I Corinthians 6:9, 10: _____

45. List the principles of giving suggested by I Corinthians 16:2.

a. _____

b. _____

c. _____

d. _____

B. Make a list of principles from the previous verses that will guide you in your attitude toward, desire for, acquisition of, and use of money.

1. There are many things more valuable than gold (Matt. 16:26; Luke 12:15; Prov. 15:16, 17).
2. Covetousness and discontentment are sins (Heb. 13:5; I Cor. 6:9, 10).
3. God is the one who gives man the ability to make money (Deut. 8:18; I Chron. 29:12).
4. Heavenly treasure is to be more desired than earthly treasure (Matt. 6:19, 20).
5. God usually rewards hard work (Prov. 13:11; 14:23).
6. Everything I have belongs to God (I Chron. 29:11). Christian stewardship is total, not partial.

7. Giving to the Lord's work is a privilege and an investment, not merely a duty or obligation (II Cor. 9:6-12; Phil. 4:11-19).

8. _____

_____

9. _____

_____

10. _____

_____

11. _____

_____

12. _____

_____

13. _____

_____

14. _____

_____

15. _____

_____

16. _____

_____

17. _____

_____

C. Do a financial profile and make a budget.
  1. Assets
     a. Salary per month   _____

     b. Additional income   _____

                 Total   _____
  2. Liabilities
     a. Outstanding debts (total) _____
     b. Itemize regular monthly obligations
        (1) Churches, ministries _____

        (2) Taxes _____
        (3) Food and
            household items _____
        (4) House payments
            or rent _____
        (5) Electricity, heat,
            water, telephone _____
        (6) Clothing and its
            maintenance _____

        (7) Insurance _____
        (8) Recreation and
            vacation _____
        (9) Savings and
            investments _____

       (10) Payment of debts _____

       (11) Medical _____

       (12) Gifts _____

       (13) Hospitality _____

       (14) Reading material _____

       (15) Education _____

       (16) Allowances _____

       (17) Automobile _____

       (18) Helping others _____

       (19) Emergencies _____

        Monthly total _____
                Total _____

Compare total monthly assets with liabilities. If your liabilities are greater than your assets, you must plan how and when you will reduce your obligations or how you can increase your income. Decide what you will do and write out your plan.

D. Develop a solution to the following matters.

1. Your living standard: _____

_____

2. Credit buying and charge accounts: _____

_____

3. Spending for recreation, gifts, and vacations: _____

_____

4. Giving to the church: _____

_____

5. Children's future education: _____

_____

6. Insurance plans: _____

_____

7. Making a will: _____

_____

8. Savings and investments: _____

_____

9. Paying bills on time: _____

_____

10. A good system of bookkeeping: _____

_____

11. How will you decide when to make major purchases such as another automobile or new furniture? _____

_____

FRIENDSHIP

Study the following verses and write down everything they have to say about being a friend, making friends, and keeping friends. Write down specifically where you are failing and plan how you will change.

Mark 10:28-30: _____

_____

Luke 16:9: _____

_____

Proverbs 25:8: _____

_____

Proverbs 25:9: _____

_____

Proverbs 25:21: _____

_____

Proverbs 25:22: _____

_____

Proverbs 11:12: _____

_____

Proverbs 14:20: _____

_____

Proverbs 14:21: _____

_____

Proverbs 21:10: _____

_____

Proverbs 3:27, 28: _____

_____

Proverbs 12:26: _____

_____

Proverbs 19:6: _____

_____

Proverbs 18:24: _____

_____

Proverbs 22:11: _____

_____

Proverbs 17:17: _____

_____

Proverbs 27:10: _____

_____

Proverbs 27:6: _____

_____

Proverbs 27:9: _____

_____

Proverbs 27:17: _____

_____

Proverbs 29:5: _____

_____

Proverbs 28:23: _____

_____

Proverbs 25:17: _____

_____

Proverbs 25:20: _____

_____

Proverbs 27:14: _____

_____

Proverbs 26:18: _____

Proverbs 26:19: _____

Proverbs 16:28: _____

Proverbs 17:9: _____

Proverbs 25:15: _____

Proverbs 15:1: _____

I Corinthians 9:19-23: _____

Acts 20:35: _____

Philippians 2:1-4: _____

Philippians 2:20-22: _____

Philippians 2:25-30: _____

Romans 12:9-21: _____

Romans 15:1, 2: _____

Romans 16:1-6: _____

John 15:13-15: _____

_____

Philippians 4:8: _____

_____

I Peter 3:8: _____

_____

II Timothy 1:14-16: _____

_____

I Corinthians 13:4-8: _____

_____

Proverbs 15:13: _____

_____

Proverbs 17:22: _____

_____

Hebrews 10:24: _____

_____

Proverbs 27:17: _____

_____

James 4:4: _____

_____

II John 10: _____

_____

Amos 3:3: _____

_____

II Corinthians 6:14-18: _____

_____

85

GUIDANCE

Knowing the Will of God

Prepared by Wayne A. Mack and Raymond Richards.

A. List some of the specific situations in which you want to determine the will of God.

_____

_____

_____

What have you done to determine God's will? _____

_____

_____

B. What comforting fact about knowing God's will is presented by these verses?

Proverbs 3:5, 6: _____

Psalm 32:8: _____

Psalm 23:1-3: _____

Isaiah 58:11: _____

C. What are the conditions for divine guidance?

Psalm 32:1-7: _____

Psalm 25:7: _____

II Corinthians 5:17: _____

II Timothy 3:16, 17: _____

Psalm 119:105: _____

Psalm 119:24: _____

Psalm 37:31: _____

Romans 12:1, 2: _____

Matthew 6:33: _____

I Corinthians 6:20: _____

Colossians 3:17: _____

Romans 8:9: _____

Romans 8:14: _____

Do you have a right relationship with God? Have you been born again by the Spirit of God, trusted in Christ as your only Saviour from your sins, and are you continuing to follow Him as Lord?

_____

_____

Are there areas of unconfessed sin and stubborn resistance to the clear teaching of the Word of God? (Example: Insisting on marrying a non-Christian)

_____

_____

Are you sincerely interested in determining the will of God, no matter what the cost may be? _____

_____

D. Read the following verses and note some of the specific areas in which the Bible provides guidance.

Psalm 37:23: _____

Proverbs 16:3: _____

Isaiah 48:17: _____

Acts 16:6-10: _____

I Thessalonians 4:3: _____

I Peter 2:15: _____

Genesis 24:40-45: _____

Ephesians 5:22, 25: _____

Ephesians 6:4: _____

Ephesians 5:3, 4: _____

Titus 2:9, 10: _____

II Corinthians 9:6, 7: _____

II Corinthians 6:14: _____

Hebrews 13:4: _____

James 4:13-16: _____

This is by no means an exhaustive list, but it will help to demonstrate how the Bible can be our guide on very practical issues.

Assignment: Using a Bible concordance, study the passages of Scripture which relate directly to your situation. Write out on a separate sheet of paper what they indicate about your area of concern.

E. The Bible provides specific help in determining His will in many situations. However, there are other situations where God does not give specific directives. Yet the Bible shows us how to proceed at such times.

   1. Write out what the following verses suggest about how to know the will of God.

Psalm 25:4, 5: _____

Psalm 27:11: _____

Psalm 5:8: _____

Genesis 24:12-14: _____

Colossians 4:23: _____

I Thessalonians 3:10: _____

Ephesians 6:18, 20: _____

Mark 11:24: _____

James 1:5: _____

How does Acts 10:1-20 illustrate this truth? _____

_____

_____

_____

Before you go to God in prayer, write down your specific requests. If one is a matter that is clearly pointed out in Scripture, then ask God to give you grace and the willingness to obey—but do obey. If the Scripture does not speak directly to the issue, write out the pros and cons on a sheet of paper and then pray. The psalmist said, ". . . I will *order* my prayer before thee and eagerly watch" (Ps. 5:2).

2. Write out what the following verses have to suggest about coming to know the will of God.

Proverbs 12:15: _____

Proverbs 15:22: _____

Proverbs 20:18: _____

Proverbs 24:6: _____

How does Acts 21:17-26 illustrate this principle? _____

_____

_____

To whom can you go who is of honest report, full of the Holy Spirit and wisdom? Your pastor? A Christian friend? Your parents? Schedule a time when you can meet with that person, having on hand as many of the facts as practical to relate to him, and then ask his honest evaluation and advice. For further help in this matter, study I Kings 12:1-20 to discover how a refusal to listen to sound advice brought hardship in the personal lives of many Israelites and division in the nation of Israel as a whole.

3. Write out what the following verses suggest about discovering God's will.

I Corinthians 16:8, 9: _____

Genesis 50:20: _____

Genesis 45:5-8: _____

Galatians 6:10: _____

Revelation 3:8, 9: _____

John 7:1: _____

Philippians 1:12-14: _____

Psalm 119:67: _____

Ecclesiastes 7:13-14: _____

Circumstances are not an infallible guide in determining the will of God for your particular situation. However, circumstances may be used to buttress the inward persuasion of the Holy Spirit and to solidify the specific Biblical principles relating to the situation. Make a list of circumstances which may indicate a "door-opening" or a "door-closing" in your life.

Door-Openers   *Door-Closers*

_____   _____

_____   _____

_____   _____

_____   _____

After you have made your list, study specific passages of Scripture that have a direct bearing on your decision. While it is true that God providentially arranges circumstances in our lives in order to direct us according to His will, circumstances may be misinterpreted. That is why it is of utmost importance to wait upon God and have a Biblical confirmation of your course of action. God has given us His Word as an authoritative guide to evaluate circumstantial evidence.

4. Write out what the following verses teach about discerning the will of God.

   Proverbs 16:3: _____

   Proverbs 16:9: _____

   I Corinthians 2:12, 14: _____

   Romans 12:2: _____

   Ephesians 5:17: _____

   II Timothy 1:7: _____ _____

   I Peter 1:13: _____

   Luke 15:17: _____

   Psalm 119:59: _____

When you became a Christian, the Bible says you received a "new mind" (Eph. 4:23). The Holy Spirit enlightens your mind so that you may be constantly transformed into the likeness of Jesus Christ. God brings circumstances into your life to make you more fruitful inwardly by manifesting the fruit of the Holy Spirit, and also outwardly by tangible evidence of God's blessing. While humbly submitting your thoughts to God and asking Him for His guidance (Prov. 16:3), fill out the following decision guide.

What are the facts about the situation? Make sure you have all the necessary information (Prov. 18:13; 16:3; 18:17; 20:25; II Tim. 1:7).

1. _____

2. _____

3. _____

4. _____

5. _____

6. _____

What alternative courses of action could I take? What would be the possible results of each alternative? What are the dangers of each course? What are the possible advantages?

Possible alternatives

1. _____

2. _____

3. _____

Possible advantages and disadvantages of each alternative
(Take into account the spiritual, social, physical,
financial, educational advantages of each alternative.)

	Pluses	*Minuses*
Plan 1		
Plan 2		
Plan 3		

Before you come to a definite decision, evaluate all the pluses and minuses. Here is a list of some specific questions you should ask yourself before you make a decision.

1. Am I running from a situation rather than patiently trusting God to work

   it out? (Ps. 11:1): _____

2. Will my decision bring increased opportunities for Christian service?

   (I Thess 2:17–3:2): _____

3. Have I really prayed about the matter, and have I really desired to know and do God's will, no matter how much personal sacrifice is involved?

   _____

4. Have I seriously considered the outcome of my decision? _____

   _____

5. Will my decision bring reproach upon God, or will it glorify Him? _____

_____

6. Will my decision be for the good of God's people? _____

_____

7. Do I have all the facts? _____

8. Have I really considered all the alternatives? Advantages and disadvantages? _____

After you have committed the matter to God in prayer and have respectfully and reverently brought all the facts to God, asking for His help (Eccles. 5:1, 2), and after you have discussed the situation with a mature Christian(s), choose one alternative which is most consistent with Biblical principles and beneficial to you and others. Write out your decision and plan of action.

My decision and plan of action is _____

_____

_____

_____

Conclusion:

Much more could be said about the matter of discerning the will of God. It is an important and very profound subject, which could involve and merit long hours of research. This brief study, however, should be sufficient to help you to learn a Biblical approach to decision making. Should you desire to do more study in this area, the following helps are recommended.

Three messages on cassette tapes by Dr. Wayne Mack, entitled "Knowing the Will of God." Cost—$3.00 per tape plus $.75 for handling and mailing. Order from the Christian Counseling & Educational Foundation, 1790 E. Willow Grove Ave., Laverock, Pa. 19118.

An article by Dr. Howard Eyrich and Pastor Bruce Strickland entitled "Counseling the Decision Makers," *The Journal of Pastoral Practice,* vol. I, no. 2, Presbyterian and Reformed Publishing Co., P.O. Box 817, Phillipsburg, N. J. 08865.

Booklets:

Guidance: Some Biblical Principles, by Oliver Barclay, InterVarsity Press.

Guidance and Wisdom, Dr. J. I. Packer, Evangelical Press.

The Mode of Guidance, by Pastor Peter Masters, The Sword & Trowel, Elephant & Castle, London.

INFERIORITY JUDGMENTS

Prepared by Wayne Mack and Raymond Richards.

A. These sentences describe ways inferiority may manifest itself. Underline the predicate (or predicates) which best describes you:

I . . . am afraid to make decisions, am very concerned about what others may think about me, act like a clown, boast about my achievements, want to be the center of attention, spend money lavishly to impress others, am defensive, am slow to admit my mistakes, blameshift, am embarrassed when others compliment and commend me, am a "know-it-all," go along with the attitudes and ideas of my peers even when I don't agree with them, go places to win the attention and approval of others, wishfully compare myself with others, am afraid to speak out in a group, like to be a "dare-devil," don't like new situations, like to be the "life of the party."

Read the following verses and write out what should be the chief purpose in life for every Christian.

Matthew 6:33: _____

I Peter 4:11: _____

I Corinthians 10:31: _____

Colossians 3:17: _____

B. With these Scriptures in mind, should self-acceptance or achieving better self-esteem and happiness be the primary purpose of your life? Is it Biblical to have this attitude, "Nothing matters as long as I am happy"? Why/why not?

_____

_____

_____

C. Read the following quote from Jay Adams' *Christian Counselors Manual* and react to it. Do you agree or disagree? List your reasons for agreeing or disagreeing.

"When Christ said that the whole law could be summed up in two commandments (love for God and love for one's neighbor), He intended to say exactly that and nothing else. Yet some Christians (with a psychologizing bent) and some psychiatrists who are Christians are not satisfied with that; they (dan-

93

gerously) add a third commandment: love yourself. They claim that unless one first learns to love himself properly he will never learn to love his neighbor, for Christ (quoting Leviticus 19:18) distinctly commands: 'Love your neighbor as your self. . . .' The concept of self-love espoused by psychologizers of the Scriptures runs counter to the expressed principle that is repeated throughout the Bible in one form or another: that one's self-esteem and what he receives for himself is the by-product of that which he gives in love to another. 'It is more blessed to give than to receive,' 'He who loses his life shall save it,' and 'Seek ye first the kingdom of God and his righteousness and all of these things shall be added to you' represent the consistent theme of the Scriptures. Self-love is nowhere either commanded or commended." Write out your response.

_____

_____

_____

_____

D. Make a list of reasons why you think people judge themselves to be inferior.

_____   _____

_____   _____

_____   _____

_____   _____

E. Read the following verses and discover how God demonstrates the value He has placed on unfallen, fallen, and redeemed man.

Genesis 1:26: _____

Genesis 9:6: _____

Psalm 8:5-8: _____

Matthew 16:26: _____

John 3:16: _____

I Peter 1:18-19: _____

I Peter 3:18: _____

I John 4:10: _____

Romans 3:23, 24: _____

Romans 5:8: _____

94

Are you a Christian? Have you truly repented of your sins and believed in Jesus Christ as the only Savior from your sins? Do you understand that good works cannot merit the favor of God and cannot be the means of salvation? Are you presently continuing to obey Him as Lord by desiring to live obediently to God's commands, studying the Word, worshiping in a church where the Scriptures are believed and taught, praying, and out of love for Christ desiring that every area of your life be controlled by Him through His Word?

_____

_____

_____

_____

F. Look at these verses and write out what is true of every Christian.

John 3:16: _____

John 5:24: _____

Romans 6:8: _____

Romans 6:14: _____

Romans 8:1: _____

Romans 8:37: _____

II Corinthians 5:7: _____

Ephesians 1:3: _____

Ephesians 1:7: _____

Philippians 4:10: _____

Philippians 4:13: _____

I John 5:4: _____

Psalm 32:1, 2: _____

Isaiah 43:25: _____

Micah 7:19: _____

Ephesians 2:5-7: _____

Ephesians 2:18-21: _____

Ephesians 2:13-14: _____

I Corinthians 6:19: _____

Romans 8:14-16, 26: _____

_____

II Timothy 1:7: _____

I Peter 2:9, 10: _____

Revelation 1:5, 6: _____

_____

Because of the tremendous things God has done for the Christian, what kind of an image can the Christian have toward himself? Positive or negative? Should the Christian go around demeaning himself? Is this a mark of spirituality?

_____

_____

G. How do you regard your physical appearance? What do you like or dislike about yourself? Is there anything about the way you look that really bothers you? In what specific ways can you improve your appearance or physical condition?

_____

_____

Assignment: Make a list of the changeable features (physical or personality traits) about yourself that you don't like. Example: "Nobody wants to be around me because I am always talking about myself." How will you improve?

H. Make a list of the unchangeable features about yourself that you wish you could change. Example: "I wish I had curly hair rather than straight hair." Thank God for the way He has made you and thank Him specifically for each unchangeable feature that you have found difficult to accept. Consider the implications of Psalm 139:13-16 in reference to your unchangeable features. List everything the psalmist says about himself.

_____

_____

Have you ever done what the psalmist did in verse 14? _____

What was he doing? _____

Dissatisfaction with our unchangeable features is an indication of a wrong perspective about how God works and a sign of ingratitude to God. Why is this true? Do you see the connection between your inferiority judgments and this statement?

_____

_____

I. Read Mark 8:34-37. Who should be at the center of the Christian's life and

thoughts? _____

How did Paul identify himself in the following verses?

Romans 8:1: _____

I Corinthians 1:1: _____

Galatians 1:10: _____

Ephesians 4:1: _____

I Timothy 1:1: _____

Do you seek to establish your worth or value by position, rank, wealth, achieve-

ments, degrees, etc.? _____

_____

What conclusion did the Apostle Paul come to after having had much reason to boast in rank, class, accomplishments, family heritage, nationality? (Phil.

3:7, 8) _____

_____

J. Make a list of the things you value most. Number them in order of priority.

Do you value the things God values? _____

1. _____   6. _____

2. _____   7. _____

3. _____   8. _____

4. _____   9. _____

5. _____   10. _____

K. Make a list of your goals—short range, medium range, and long range. Are they realistic? Can they be fulfilled? Are they goals God would approve? Ask some godly person to evaluate your goals. Write out specific plans to fulfill each goal.

L. Answer the following question five times. Who are you?

I am . . . _____

_____

_____

_____

_____

M. What is God's way of discovering a life which is both pleasing to Him and personally fulfilling? (Mark 8:35) _____

_____

What is the result of making one's own selfish concerns the number one priority? (Mark 8:35, 36) _____

_____

What do these verses indicate about the way to overcome judgments of inferiority? _____

_____

_____

Do you want to be a Christian because you love God and want to obey Him, or so that God can gratify your psychological needs? _____

_____

N. *Assignment:* Make a list of the ways you are seeking to "save your life" by drawing attention to yourself. Example: "I don't want to be just a violinist—I want to be the conductor!" or, "I am going to read all those philosophy books in order to appear intelligent." Ask God to forgive you for your self-centeredness and then seek to change by using your abilities to serve other people.

O. After reading the following verses, what one word describes Biblical love? John 3:16; Galatians 2:20; Ephesians 5:25; Acts 20:35; Romans 12:20.

_____

In your attempt to "give" and to achieve, are you overextending yourself? Are you attempting to do things that you are not able to do? Are you attempting to do things which require more intellectual or physical ability than God has given you? In II Corinthians 10:14, Paul was careful to mention that he did not overextend himself. In Romans 12:3, Paul also noted the value of every Christian having an honest estimation of his gifts and limitations. Using Romans 12:6-8, list the gifts and abilities God has given you. Then, using Romans 12:9-21, list the specific ways you will use these gifts to serve other people. Ask someone to evaluate each of your lists. Examples: God has given me the gift of cheerfulness; I'll go over and visit Mrs. Jones in the hospital. God has given me the gift of helpfulness; I'll go over and help my neighbor tune his car.

_____

_____

_____

_____

_____

_____

_____

P. *Summary:* To overcome inferiority, my chief goal and concern in life is

_____.

Because I am a Christian, my true identity is found in _____.

God has given me the Holy Spirit to live the abundant life in Christ. Part of this abundant life is found in using my gifts and resources to _____

_____. As a result, Jesus Christ has

promised me (John 15:11) _____.

INTERPERSONAL RELATIONSHIPS
You can be a nice person.—Philippians 4:5

The Greek word ἐπιεικές used in Philippians 4:5 means forbearing, large hearted, gentle, courteous, considerate, generous, lenient, moderate. In summary it is describing a quality which is the opposite of irritability, rudeness, and abrasiveness; it is describing a quality that would make a person nice instead of nasty: it is saying that if you are a Christian, you can be a nice person.

1. With whom or what are you most likely to be irritable? What is there about your surroundings that irritates you? About yourself? About your friends, associates, family? When are you most likely to be irritable? How do you express irritability?

2. Identify the last three times you became irritated and analyze what happened and what you did. If you can't remember three instances from the past, examine several times when you are prone to be irritated in the present and future.

3. Examine the following items and circle the things that tend to irritate you: when you don't get your own way; when others don't do what you want them to do; when others make mistakes; when others are slow to understand, appreciate or accept your point of view; when others don't give you the respect or attention you desire; when others disagree with you, or criticize or oppose or rebuke or correct you; when others fail or are inefficient; when others insist on having their own way; when others won't cooperate with you or yield to you; when others won't leave you alone; when others deny you your rights; when you don't get what you want; when others interfere with your plans; when others will not change as you want them to change; when you don't get the promotion or position or grades you desire; when others say "no" to you; when others ignore you or treat others better than they treat you. Ask your mate or a close friend to evaluate you in terms of this list.

4. In the light of the previous assignments, make a list of specific ways in which you need to change to become a more forbearing, nicer person.

5. Study the following passages and notice how the people described reacted in potentially irritating circumstances. How would you have reacted in these instances? Did they manifest forbearance or irritability?

Genesis 4:1-14: _____

Genesis 13:5-13: _____

Genesis 30:1, 2: _____

Genesis 45:1-15: _____

I Kings 12:6-15: _____

John 13:1-17: _____

Luke 9:51-56: _____

Matthew 15:21-28: _____

Matthew 20:17-24 (esp. vs. 24): _____

Matthew 18:23-35: _____

John 13:21-30: _____

John 21:15-19: _____

Acts 11:1-18: _____

Acts 13:50-52: _____

Acts 7:54-60: _____

Acts 16:19-34: _____

6. Study the following verses and note what you must do to overcome irritability:

John 17:17: _____

Acts 20:32: _____

II Timothy 3:15-17: _____

Colossians 1:9-11: _____

Proverbs 16:32; 29:11: _____

I Timothy 4:7: _____

Proverbs 19:11: _____

Proverbs 27:12: _____

Proverbs 28:28: _____

Proverbs 19:19: _____

James 1:2-5: _____

Philippians 1:12-19: _____

Proverbs 22:24, 25: _____

Romans 8:28, 29: _____

101

Romans 5:3-5: _____

James 4:6: _____

Ephesians 5:20: _____

I Corinthians 10:13: _____

7. Focus on several ways in which you need to change to become a nicer person, make these items a constant matter of prayer, refuse to excuse yourself when you fail, confess your sins daily, and discipline yourself to work daily on becoming a more forbearing person. If you are a Christian and do this consistently, you will become a nicer person and become a better testimony for Christ.

Study Guide for Healing Broken Relationships
Philippians 4:2, 3

Philippians 4:2, 3 indicates that Euodias and Syntyche had once gotten along well, but something had happened to break the close relationship between the two of them.

1. Make a list of several people with whom you do not have as good a relationship as you once did. (These people might include your husband or wife, a child, your parents, your neighbor, your pastor, a church member, your boss, etc.)
2. Study Philippians 4:2, 3 and list several things that Euodias and Syntyche had in common. Now make a list of what you have in common with the people you listed under assignment number 1. (Example: live in same home, neighborhood; attend same church, are Christians, etc.)
3. Use your sanctified imagination and list some possible causes for the break in the relationship between Euodias and Syntyche. Now make a specific list of what caused the rift between you and the people previously mentioned. (Example: He criticized me; he ignored me; he disagreed with me; etc.)
4. Problems between us and others become enlarged when we handle them in a wrong way. Study the following Scripture verses and record what should not be done when a problem arises between you and another person.

Proverbs 15:1: _____

Proverbs 29:11, 20, 22: _____

Romans 12:17, 19: _____

Ephesians 4:25-27: _____

Ephesians 4:29-30: _____

Colossians 3:8, 9: _____

James 4:1, 2, 11: _____

I Peter 2:1: _____

I Peter 3:8, 9: _____

5. Study Philippians 4:2, 3 and answer the following questions:
   a. How do these verses encourage us to think that fractured relationships can be healed?
   b. What does the fact that Paul speaks to both people indicate about solving interpersonal relationships? List how you would have been at fault in reference to the people previously mentioned.

c. What does it mean to "be of the same mind in the Lord"? Study Philippians 2:1-8 before you answer this question. Study Matthew 5:21-48; Luke 6:32-35; Romans 12:17, 18, 20, 21; Colossians 3:12-16; I Corinthians 13:4-8; I Peter 2:18–3:6, 8, 9; Proverbs 15:1; 16:24, 32; 17:14, 27, 28; 18:6, 7, 8, 23; 20:3; 21:23; 25:15; 29:11 and make a list of what God wants you to do and how you may serve the other people to whom you are not as close.

d. According to Philippians 4:3, what is often needed to solve interpersonal conflicts? (Also study Prov. 12:15; 11:14; 15:22; Rom. 15:14; Gal. 6:1, 2.) Plan now from whom you will seek God's kind of help and make an appointment to seek counsel.

LIFE-DOMINATING SINS

Drunkenness, Drug Addiction, Homosexuality

People with these problems need total re-structuring. Drunkenness, drug addiction, and homosexuality are life-dominating sins; they usually affect every area of life.

1. These problems are sin (I Cor. 6:9, 10; Gal. 5:19-21).
2. These problems are life-dominating sins (Eph. 5:18; I Cor. 6:12; Deut. 21:21; Prov. 20:1; 7:6-23; 23:29-35; Isa. 5:11, 13, 22; Joel 3:3; 1:5; Amos 6:6; Hosea 4:11). They often affect a person's—

   a. Eating habits
   b. Home relationships
   c. Sleep
   d. Job
   e. Friends (social life)
   f. Church attendance and service
   g. Emotions (self-pity, anger)
   h. Economics (finances)
   i. Health
   j. Character and practices (deceitfulness)
   k. Marriage and family life

The drunkard, homosexual, drug addict are insecure, unhappy people who are looking for satisfaction. They often do not know how to cope with life and are riddled with guilt. They turn to the bottle or drugs for quick satisfaction. For example, when Joe performs poorly at work, he feels bad, so he turns to the bottle for satisfaction. Then he performs worse and feels worse. So he drinks again, and consequently his health suffers and his relationship with his wife becomes strained. This causes him to feel worse, and he turns again to the bottle for relief.

3. Since the problems are sin (not disease), there is hope.
   a. I John 1:7
   b. I Corinthians 6:9, 10; Romans 6:14; Ephesians 5:18
4. God's solution to life-dominating sin is the filling of the Spirit (Eph. 5:18).
   a. To be filled with the Spirit means to submit to the Spirit's directions in every area of life. It means to be filled with the right things. It means to put off the old man and put on Jesus Christ. It means restructuring your life according to God's Word. It means submitting to God's directives concerning work. It means handling your problems in a Biblical way. It means handling money in a God-appointed way. It means learning to relate to people according to the Scriptures.
   b. To be filled with the Spirit involves replacing the unbiblical behavior and attitude with Biblical behavior and attitudes (Eph. 4:17-22). It involves reorganizing and reorienting your responses into a new pattern (Rom. 6:19).
   c. It may involve probing into every area of your life to discover concrete ways you are failing God and others. Honesty and thoroughness are essential.

d. Then, having discovered the ways you are operating unbiblically, you must repent and adopt Biblical patterns. You probably will need to replace certain friendships. You must avoid all close contact and association with companions with whom you have indulged in this practice (I Cor. 15:33; Prov. 13:20). You will also have to stay away from those places frequented by people who engage in the same practice. Conversely, you will need to deepen or develop friendships with Christians who are strong in the Lord (II Tim. 2:22; Heb. 10:24, 25). Your whole life may need to be restructured: how you do your work; where and how you spend your time; how you relate to other people; how you spend your money; etc.

e. You will need to institute a meaningful program of Bible reading, prayer, Scripture memorization, and church attendance and fellowship (Ps. 119: 9, 11; John 15:3; Eph. 5:26, 27).

f. You may also need to keep a daily journal of times when you are tempted; what you do when you are tempted; where you are; with whom you are; what you are thinking about. This journal may be of immense value in overcoming your problem.

g. You may also need assistance in setting Biblical goals for living and in attaining them.

h. You should establish a regular schedule, making sure you have time for all your God-given responsibilities.

i. You must devise a specific plan to use whenever you are tempted and put that plan into practice immediately and regularly when the temptation comes (Rom. 12:17). You must exercise (discipline) yourself for the purpose of godliness (I Tim. 4:7).

LONELINESS

How to Overcome the Problem of Loneliness
Prepared by Wayne Mack and Raymond Richards.

The problem of loneliness has reached epidemic proportions in our day. Psychiatrist Paul Tournier said that loneliness is ". . . the most devastating malady of this age." On the Personal Data Inventory sheets that are filled out by our counselees, the problem of loneliness is mentioned as being one of the most serious problems they face. Loneliness affects people of every age, sex, social standing, etc. Loneliness is a universal problem.

God has created us as social creatures (Gen. 2:18). As social creatures, we naturally have the desire and capacity for fellowship, and we cannot be happy unless this basic need is met. The problem of loneliness often has two aspects and will not be solved unless both of these aspects are considered. The problem of loneliness often has a human and a divine dimension. The feeling of loneliness, then, is a symptom of a deeper problem. It often arises because a person does not have or maintain a proper relationship with God and with other people.

Loneliness is often associated with a deficient relationship to God.

A. Study the following verses and note how sin severs our relationship with God.

Deuteronomy 32:19-20: _____

Psalm 66:18: _____

Proverbs 15:29: _____

Isaiah 59:2: _____

Ephesians 2:12: _____

Ephesians 4:17-19: _____

Titus 3:3: _____

B. Study the following verses and note the way that God restores sinful, alienated man to Himself.

Colossians 1:20, 22: _____

I Peter 3:18: _____

Romans 3:24: _____

Ephesians 1:7: _____

Ephesians 2:13-16: _____

Hebrews 9:26-28: _____

Romans 5:1: _____

John 1:12: _____

Are you a Christian? Have you trusted in Jesus Christ as the only Savior for

your sins, and do you desire to follow Him as Lord? _____
If you are not a Christian, then you need to realize that your loneliness is the
result of your alienation from God. There is a God-shaped vacuum within that
can be fulfilled only by God, your Creator and Sustainer. That vacuum will
never really be filled until you come in repentance and faith to receive forgiveness of sins through Him.

C. What special promises does God give to and fulfill in the lives of Christians who
faithfully trust Him in every circumstance?

Joshua 1:9: _____

Psalm 23:4: _____

Psalm 27:10: _____

Isaiah 49:15: _____

Psalm 90:1: _____

Psalm 71:9, 18: _____

Psalm 139:6-12: _____

Isaiah 43:2: _____

Philippians 4:19: _____

Matthew 28:20: _____

Romans 8:38, 39: _____

Describe the specific way in which Paul experienced these truths (II Tim. 4:9,

10, 16, 17): _____

_____

What tremendous resources has God given to Christians so that they may be

sufficient in any and every circumstance? (II Pet. 1:2, 3): _____

_____

Augustine, the great theologian and church father, said, "God has made us for Himself and our hearts are restless until they rest in Him."

Suggested Assignment: Answer the following questions as specifically as possible.

When are you most prone to feel lonely? _____

_____

_____

How should you react when you begin to feel this way? _____

_____

_____

D. Having come to Jesus Christ and having been forgiven of his sins, how may a person develop and maintain a deep sense of the presence of God? Study the following verses and note how the Bible instructs us in developing a closer walk with God.

Exodus 33:12-16: _____

_____

Psalm 116:3, 4: _____

Psalm 119:9, 11: _____

Psalm 119:104: _____

Psalm 66:18: _____

Psalm 34:18: _____

Psalm 46:10: _____

John 14:21, 23: _____

Hebrews 4:14-16: _____

Hebrews 10:20-25: _____

_____

Jude 20, 21: _____

John 7:37-39: _____

Psalm 119:2, 3: _____

Colossians 3:16: _____

Psalm 4:4: _____

Ephesians 3:16-19: _____

_____

Philippians 3:8-11: _____

_____

Philippians 4:6, 7: _____

I John 3:22: _____

Isaiah 41:10: _____

Isaiah 57:15: _____

Isaiah 66:2: _____

Ephesians 2:18: _____

II Corinthians 6:14-18: _____

James 4:8: _____

John 15:1-7: _____

Hebrews 13:5, 6: _____

Are there some specific areas where you are knowingly rebelling against God?

If so, what are they? _____

_____

According to Ephesians 4:22-24, you must forsake and repudiate those sinful practices in which you are engaging and replace them with Biblical habits and practices. As long as there is an unwillingness to submit to the clear teaching of the Word of God, the Holy Spirit will be grieved and fellowship with God will be hindered (Ps. 66:18).

Loneliness is often associated with a deficient relationship to other people.

A. Here is a catalog of some qualities and behaviors that hinder good relationships with other people. Put a circle around the qualities or behaviors listed below which are present in your life and may be contributing to your feeling of loneliness.

   1. Pride
   2. Hostility
   3. Fear of not being adequate
   4. Fear of being rejected
   5. Impatience and irritability

110

6. Prejudice
7. Fear of being taken advantage of
8. Suspiciousness
9. Educational and social barriers
10. Excessive dependence on other people
11. Smothering—being too demanding
12. Selfishness—self-centeredness
13. Being critical and complaining
14. Perfectionism
15. Bossiness, pushiness, officiousness
16. Moroseness, gloominess, heaviness
17. Excessive shyness or bashfulness
18. Unwillingness to compromise, change, yield, or sacrifice
19. Critical and complaining attitude
20. Having the spirit of Diotrephes. Always "wanting to have the preeminence and the first and last say among other people" (III John 9, 10).
21. Stinginess
22. Blameshifting, inconsiderateness, cruelty
23. Sloppiness
24. Gossiping
25. Deceitfulness

B. Qualities and Behaviors That Foster Good Relations and Help to Alleviate Loneliness

1. Love others unconditionally.

   a. What standard does Jesus establish that should be a Christian's guideline for loving others? (John 13:34; Rom. 5:8): _____

   _____

   b. How would you describe the "just as" kind of love?

   _____

   _____

   c. How will the world recognize that you are a true disciple of Christ? (John 13:35): _____

   d. Read John 13:34; 15:12, 17. Is loving others an optional matter?

   _____

   How should a true disciple treat his enemies? (Matt. 5:44): _____

   _____

   According to Matthew 5:48, is there ever a time when you may be

111

exempted from loving someone else? _____

_____

2. Be helpful to other people.

Read the following verses and note the specific ways in which you can serve other people.

Proverbs 3:27, 28: _____

Proverbs 18:24: _____

Proverbs 25:21, 22: _____

Acts 20:35: _____

Luke 2:36-38: _____

Matthew 5:41, 42: _____

Matthew 5:40: _____

Philippians 2:3, 4: _____

II Corinthians 1:3-5: _____

I Peter 4:9: _____

Study Philippians 2:25-30. In what specific way did Epaphroditus minister to Paul and extend himself for other Christians?

_____

What was Paul's opinion of Epaphroditus? _____

What did Paul want other Christians to think about him? _____

_____ (cf. vs. 29).

Plan specifically how you will begin to help other people. Consider your time, home, money, job, recreation, etc. How can you best serve Christ with all your abilities and resources by serving other people? Make a list of 10 practical ways you may serve other people.

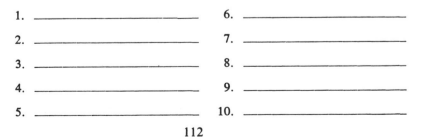

1. _____   6. _____

2. _____   7. _____

3. _____   8. _____

4. _____   9. _____

5. _____   10. _____

3. Developing the Fruit of the Spirit

   If you are a Christian, the Holy Spirit dwells in you (I Cor. 6:19). By the power of the indwelling Spirit you now have the desire and ability to become more and more like Jesus Christ. Study the following verses and note specifically the character qualities that are deficient in your life. Ask God for the strength to change where you need to change and look for opportunities and situations to "put on the new man" (Eph. 4:22).

   Galatians 5:22: _____

   _____

   Ephesians 4:2: _____

   Colossians 3:12, 13: _____

   _____

   _____

   Study I Corinthians 13:4-8. List the eight negative characteristics of love and the positive characteristics of love.

   1. _____   9. _____

   2. _____   10. _____

   3. _____   11. _____

   4. _____   12. _____

   5. _____   13. _____

   6. _____   14. _____

   7. _____   15. _____

   8. _____   16. _____

   James 3:17: _____

   Study II Peter 1:2-10. List the eight character qualities that are listed in verses 4-7.

   1. _____   5. _____

   2. _____   6. _____

   3. _____   7. _____

   4. _____   8. _____

   How is it possible for a Christian to develop these qualities? (cf. vss. 2, 3):

   _____

How should the Christian respond to the fact that he has been made a partaker of the divine nature? (cf. vss. 5, 6): _____

_____

What will be the result of diligently applying ourselves to growing in Christian character? (vs. 8): _____

_____. How does Peter describe the person who remains dormant and unwilling to make changes in his life? (vss. 8, 9): _____

If you are a lonely person, you must ponder whether or not it may be because you are not developing the fruit of the Spirit, and as a result people do not want to be around you. List the qualities that are most lacking in your life.

1. _____   2. _____

3. _____   4. _____

4. Focus on becoming the right kind of friend.
   Note: Some verses listed below describe the ways in which you should act. Others describe things you should refrain from doing if you are going to be a good friend.

   Exodus 33:11: _____

   Psalm 31:11: _____

   Psalm 38:11: _____

   Proverbs 17:17: _____

   Genesis 18:17: _____

   Proverbs 25:19: _____

   Proverbs 26:18, 19: _____

   Proverbs 16:28, 29: _____

   Proverbs 27:17: _____

   Proverbs 29:5: _____

   Proverbs 28:23: _____

   Proverbs 27:14: _____

   Ecclesiastes 4:9-12: _____

I Samuel 20:17: _____

John 13:15: _____

Proverbs 27:5, 6: _____

Proverbs 27:9, 10: _____

John 15:13-15: _____

Romans 5:1, 2: _____

I Thessalonians 2:8: _____

Hebrews 10:24: _____

James 2:23: _____

Assess your relationship with others. Have you been an example or a stumblingblock? Have you been faithful or unfaithful to your commitments? Have you communicated that you are sincerely interested in other people? Give specific examples confirming your answers. If others were describing you, would they describe you as one who is considerate, truthful, loving, loyal, etc., or would they see you as one who is aloof, suspicious,

unconcerned, all talk and no action? _____

_____

_____

5. Encourage and appreciate other people.
   Study the following verses and consider how they illustrate the need to become a more appreciative and concerned friend.

II Timothy 4:11: _____

Philemon 4, 5: _____

I Thessalonians 4:9: _____

Proverbs 25:20: _____

Proverbs 27:14: _____

Proverbs 16:24: _____

Proverbs 15:4: _____

I Corinthians 16:16, 17: _____

II Timothy 1:16: _____

Proverbs 17:9: _____

Proverbs 15:22, 23: _____

I Corinthians 1:4-6: _____

Philippians 2:19-22: _____

Revelation 2:1-3: _____

Revelation 2:18, 19: _____

Revelation 2:12, 13: _____

Revelation 3:9: _____

Notice how our Lord Jesus Christ in Revelation 2 and 3 did not notice only the peculiar problems of each church. He also commended each church for ministries and qualities which were the strong points of the particular church. Begin to emphasize the strong points of others and to lovingly commend them for their abilities and qualities that have been a blessing to you.

Make a list of ways you can encourage someone else. Make it a practice to express appreciation to someone else. Keep in mind that the difference between expressing appreciation and flattery is that expressing appreciation demonstrates a real concern for the welfare of the other person and an unselfish desire to see the other person grow and develop. Flattery, on the other hand, is a *selfish* manipulative device of insincerely complimenting someone else in order to win a favorable response from him.

6. Become vitally involved in a local church which believes and *preaches the Bible.*

God has ordained that the local church is to be one of the channels of Christian service and spiritual growth for every Christian. While it is Biblical that the church exists for the purpose of worshiping God (I Pet. 2:9) and for the purpose of evangelism (Matt. 28:19), it is equally true that the local church exists for the mutual edification of each believer. Look up the following verses and describe the kind of relationship that the early Christians had with each other. Notice the deep involvement and concern they had for one another. Note what these early believers did to and for each other.

Acts 2:44-47: _____

Acts 4:23: _____

Acts 9:36-41: _____

Acts 12:1-5: _____

Acts 14:19-28: _____

Acts 16:40: _____

116

Acts 20:17-38: _____

Acts 20:7-14: _____

Acts 28:11-15: _____

Romans 16:1, 2: _____

Romans 16:3-4: _____

Romans 16:8, 9: _____

Romans 16:13: _____

I Corinthians 16:15-18: _____

Philippians 1:3-8: _____

Philippians 2:25-30: _____

Philippians 4:10: _____

I Thessalonians 2:7-11: _____

I Thessalonians 3:5-10: _____

I Thessalonians 4:9, 10: _____

II Timothy 1:16-18: _____

Philemon 1, 2: _____

It is evident from these verses that the relationship of these early believers was extremely close and satisfying. In spite of their differences, the spiritual and social needs of these Christians were satisfied through their deep involvement with each other in the church. Are you deeply involved in and associated with other Christians in a church, or is your relationship to the church superficial and casual? What efforts have you made and what other efforts could you make to develop deep relations with other Christians? Don't wait for others to solicit your friendship. Don't demand perfection in the church or other Christians, and don't demand absolute agreement on all issues. Find a church where the Bible is preached, Christ is honored, and people are honestly seeking to live the Christian life and really become involved. Seek to be the kind of Christian brother/sister and church member described in the verses you studied earlier. As you do, you will find your spiritual and social needs being satisfied and your problem of loneliness diminishing.

Summary: If a person is to overcome the problem of loneliness, he must first of all establish and maintain a proper relationship to God through His Son Jesus Christ. One's relationship to God is maintained by studying and meditating on the Word of God, through prayer, by obedience to the Scriptures, and through Christian fellowship. But also, if one is to overcome the problem of loneliness, he must seek to establish good relationships with other people. These two dimensions of the problem can be summarized and solved by obedience to the words of Jesus when He said, "Thou shalt love the Lord thy God with all thy heart, and with all thy soul, and with all thy mind. This is the first and great commandment. And the second is like unto it, Thou shalt love thy neighbor as thyself" (Matt. 22:37-39).

LOVE

Developing True Love

The word *love* is one of the most commonly used words in our English vocabulary. Almost everyone would agree that love is one of the most important qualities of human life. We are told, "Love makes the world go round," and, "What the world needs now is love, sweet love." Without love, life becomes unbearable, relationships deteriorate, marriages fall apart, families disintegrate, and personal problems become overwhelming.

In many passages of the Word of God, Jesus Christ the Lord emphasized the importance of love. I quote only a few of the many.

1. "You shall *love* the Lord your God with all your heart, and with all your soul, and with all your mind." "You shall *love* your neighbor as yourself" (Matt. 22:37, 39).

2. "A new commandment I give unto you, that you *love* one another, even as I have loved you, that you also *love* one another. By this shall all men know that you are my disciples, if you have *love* one for another" (John 13:34, 35).

3. "*Love* your enemies, do good to those who hate you, bless those who curse you, pray for those who mistreat you" (Luke 6:27, 28).

Love, then, is not only what the world needs—it's what every person in that world needs; it's what every married person needs; it's what every parent and child needs; it's what every neighbor needs. That leads us to ask two very important questions that must be answered when we talk about love.

1. *What is love?* Ask ten different people, and you may get six different definitions of love. Or, you may get no definitions at all because many people who talk about love don't seem to have any idea what it is. This is tragic, because before we can say we love God or anyone else, we've got to know what it means to love. In this study, we want to discover what the Bible teaches about love so that we may love God and our fellow man as God wants us to love.

2. *How may we demonstrate our love to others—(husbands, wives, parents, children, neighbors, employers, employees, fellow Christians, enemies, etc.) —in specific ways?* Most of us live and love in abstractions and intangibles. As a marriage counselor, I have had many husbands and wives tell me that they loved each other, but when asked to give 10 or 15 specific ways in which they expressed their love to each other, they looked at me as if I had asked them to explain Einstein's theory of relativity. This also is tragic because love is worthless (indeed, it is non-existent) unless it is manifested in concrete, specific ways. In this study you will be asked to become very specific about your expression of love.

119

A. Look up the following verses in your Bible and write down what each of them indicates about true love. Note carefully what love isn't as well as what it is; what it doesn't do as well as what it does do. Note also the implications of these verses as well as the explicit statements. To get you started, I will suggest what you might write down for the first two Scripture verses. After that you are on your own.

1. Ephesians 5:25: Love is described in terms of actions, not feelings. Love involves sacrificing for the sake of the other person. Love focuses on doing something for the other person. Love involves meeting the needs of the other person even if it involves personal sacrifice, pain, and discomfort. Love is not what the other person does for me or to me. Love does not focus on me, but on helping the other person. Love doesn't wait for the other person to ask for help or be helpful. Love takes the initiative. Love gives even if it receives nothing in return. Love is unselfish.

2. Titus 2:3, 4: Love can be taught. Love does not just happen. (People do not "fall in love." They may fall into infatuation or a warm, tender feeling; but this warm, tender feeling is not to be equated with Biblical love. Biblical love may involve a warm, tender feeling at times, but there is much more to it than that.) Since love can be taught and learned, it involves the mind and the intellect, and not just the emotions. If a person says he or she does not love someone, that person can learn to love the other person if he really wants to.

3. Romans 5:5; Galatians 5:22, 23; II Timothy 1:7; I John 4:7 (note the source of true love, where it comes from, and how we get it):

4. Romans 13:8-10: _____

   _____

   _____

   _____

   _____

5. Romans 14:15 (the word *charity* is another word for love): _____

   _____

   _____

   _____

   _____

6. Proverbs 10:12 (note carefully what love doesn't do as well as what it does

   do): _____

   _____

7. I Corinthians 8:1: _____

_____

_____

_____

_____

8. Galatians 5:13-15 (note carefully what love doesn't do and what it does
   do; note the focus of love): _____

_____

_____

_____

_____

9. Ephesians 4:2, 15, 16: _____

_____

_____

_____

_____

10. Colossians 2:2; 3:14: _____

_____

_____

_____

_____

11. Philippians 1:9: _____

_____

_____

_____

_____

12. I Thessalonians 4:9-12: _____

_____
_____
_____
_____

13. I Timothy 1:5: _____

_____
_____
_____
_____

14. James 2:1-13 (especially note vss. 8 and 9): _____

_____
_____
_____
_____

15. I John 3:16-18: _____

_____
_____
_____
_____

16. Luke 6:27-38: _____

_____
_____
_____
_____

B. I Corinthians 13 is the great love chapter of the Bible. No discussion of what love is would be complete without a study of this chapter. Remember, Christ our Lord is the personification and perfect example of the kind of love described in this chapter. Remember also that this chapter was written to Christians; to people who were forgiven and redeemed by the atoning death of Christ; to people who were indwelt and empowered by the Holy Spirit of God. I Corinthians 13 describes God's kind of love, a kind of love which a Christian may have and express because of what God has done and is doing for him and in him. Study particularly verses 4-7 and write down the different elements of love. Then under "a" of each element list a number of antonyms to the word describing love (e.g., if the text says that love does not behave itself unseemly, you could put love is mannerly, love is courteous, love is polite). In other words, under "a" translate the negatives into positives or the positives into negatives. This will help you to understand more clearly what love is. Use a dictionary if you need help. You may also want to look at several versions of the Bible to gain a clearer understanding of what love is. After you have translated the negatives into positives or positives into negatives, give an illustration under "b" of how you will manifest this aspect of love. To get you started, I will suggest what you might write down for the first element. After that you are on your own.

1. Love suffers long, endures offenses, is patient.
    a. Antonym: Love is not impatient or nasty; love is not fretful or intolerant.
    b. Illustration: I will not be impatient with my wife when she forgets to get the car filled up with gas, even though this happens quite frequently and even though the car runs out of gas while I am on my way to the gas station.

2. _____

    a. Antonym: _____

    _____

    _____

    b. Illustration: _____

    _____

    _____

3. _____

    a. Antonym: _____

    _____

    _____

    b. Illustration: _____

    _____

    _____

4. _____

   a. Antonym: _____

      _____

      _____

   b. Illustration: _____

      _____

      _____

5. _____

   a. Antonym: _____

      _____

      _____

   b. Illustration: _____

      _____

      _____

6. _____

   a. Antonym: _____

      _____

      _____

   b. Illustration: _____

      _____

      _____

7. _____

   a. Antonym: _____

      _____

      _____

   b. Illustration: _____

      _____

      _____

8. _____

   a. Antonym: _____

   _____

   _____

   b. Illustration: _____

   _____

   _____

9. _____

   a. Antonym: _____

   _____

   _____

   b. Illustration: _____

   _____

   _____

10. _____

   a. Antonym: _____

   _____

   _____

   b. Illustration: _____

   _____

   _____

11. _____

   a. Antonym: _____

   _____

   _____

   b. Illustration: _____

   _____

   _____

12. _____

   a. Antonym: _____

     _____

     _____

   b. Illustration: _____

     _____

     _____

13. _____

   a. Antonym: _____

     _____

     _____

   b. Illustration: _____

     _____

     _____

14. _____

   a. Antonym: _____

     _____

     _____

   b. Illustration: _____

     _____

     _____

C. Make a list of the legitimate desires and longings of other people (whomever you want to love in a Biblical fashion—your wife, husband, mother, neighbor, father, child, etc.). Think of the other person's total life—physical, intellectual, spiritual, social, emotional, financial, recreational, etc. We have seen that love involves helping other people, but you probably won't really help unless you know how they need help. Consideration is usually a prerequisite for helping people. What are the legitimate desires and longings of other people?

1. Companionship

2. Encouragement

3. Spiritual growth

4. Spiritual stimulation

5. Wise counsel   13. _____

6. A good example   14. _____

7. Acceptance and appreciation   15. _____

8. A close relationship with God   16. _____

9. _____   17. _____

10. _____   18. _____

11. _____   19. _____

12. _____   20. _____

D. Write down what you are doing to serve other people. Add to that list other specific things that you might do. Make an immediate and continuous effort to put your lists into practice.

1. _____

2. _____

3. _____

4. _____

5. _____

6. _____

7. _____

8. _____

9. _____

10. _____

11. _____

12. _____

13. _____

14. _____

15. _____

16. _____

17. _____

18. _____

127

19. _____

20. _____

21. _____

22. _____

23. _____

24. _____

25. _____

26. _____

27. _____

28. _____

29. _____

30. _____

31. _____

32. _____

33. _____

34. _____

35. _____

36. _____

37. _____

38. _____

39. _____

40. _____

41. _____

42. _____

43. _____

44. _____

45. _____

46. _____

47. _____

48. _____

49. _____

50. _____

51. _____

52. _____

53. _____

OVEREATING (OBESITY)

Study the following verses and note everything they have to say about overindulgence. Write down everything these verses say about the person who overeats: what his overeating may indicate about him; what may be the result of his overeating; and how he may overcome this problem. Some of the verses relate directly to the problem; others contain principles that may be applied. Memorize several verses that relate to the problem and devise a plan for overcoming it. Write out your plan in an orderly fashion and put it into practice. Some specific suggestions are included after the Bible verses.

A. Bible Verses

Exodus 16:8-21: _____

Numbers 11:4, 32-33: _____

Deuteronomy 21:20, 21: _____

Judges 3:21, 22: _____

I Samuel 2:12-17: _____

Psalm 104:14, 15: _____

Proverbs 21:20, 21: _____

Proverbs 23:1-3, 19-21: _____

Proverbs 28:7: _____

Isaiah 5:11, 12, 22: _____

Isaiah 22:12, 13: _____

Habakkuk 2:4, 5: _____

Amos 6:4-7: _____

Luke 12:19, 20, 45, 46: _____

Luke 21:34: _____

Luke 9:23: _____

Romans 13:11-14; 14:13: _____

I Corinthians 6:12, 13; 10:13: _____

I Corinthians 9:27; 10:31; 11:21: _____

II Corinthians 7:1; 1:11: _____

Galatians 5:19-24: _____

Ephesians 4:19; 5:18: _____

Philippians 3:18, 19; 4:10-13; 1:19: _____

Colossians 3:17: _____

I Timothy 4:3-5, 7: _____

I Peter 4:1-3: _____

Jude 12: _____

Hebrews 4:14-16; 10:24, 25: _____

B. Specific Suggestions
   1. Review Scriptural insights daily.
   2. Memorize Scripture and repeat it out loud when tempted.
   3. Pray for divine help daily, and especially when tempted.
   4. Ask others to pray for you and check up on you regularly.
   5. Enlist the help of your family.
   6. Do not have junk food around the house.
   7. Prepare only enough food.
   8. Serve the food in the kitchen.
   9. Weigh yourself every four days.
   10. Keep a daily journal of all the food you eat and how much.
   11. Stop fast eating; put forks down between bites.
   12. Never shop when you are hungry.
   13. Choose only one place to eat and never eat anywhere else in your house.
   14. Put high calorie foods out of sight.
   15. Put Bible verses or other warnings on the refrigerator or elsewhere.
   16. Learn how to handle your problems Scripturally; find other legitimate ways of getting satisfaction.
   17. Analyze what is happening; keep a daily journal of *when* most likely to overeat, with whom most likely to overeat, what you are doing or what is happening or what problems you are facing or what you are thinking about when you are tempted to overeat.
   18. Observe thinner people and notice how well they look.
   19. Observe yourself and notice how sloppy you look.
   20. Deal with your overeating as a sin.
   21. Remind yourself of the health hazards of overweight.
   22. Remind yourself regularly of the benefits of being thinner. You'll feel better, look better, have more energy and confidence.
   23. Plan some exciting reward for yourself if you succeed.
   24. Follow the counsel of Robert Smith, M.D., to eat with the correct frequency (only three times a day), the correct amount of food, and the correct kinds of food.

131

PLANNING AND PRIORITIES

Time, Talents, and Goals

Parts of this study were developed by Pastor Timothy Keller.

One of the biggest struggles a Christian will have during his or her life concerns the determining of *priorities*. Many things will demand the use of his time and talents. A Christian must decide how best to use his time and talents; how to discern the things that are excellent (Phil. 1:10); how to make the best use of his opportunities (Eph. 5:16). He must prayerfully, Scripturally, and submissively plan his use of time and talents and then submit it all to God for His approval or disapproval (Prov. 16:3; James 4:13-16; Rom. 1:13). Usually those who fail to plan are planning to fail.

A. Study the following Scriptures and note what they suggest about the use of time, planning, and establishing priorities.

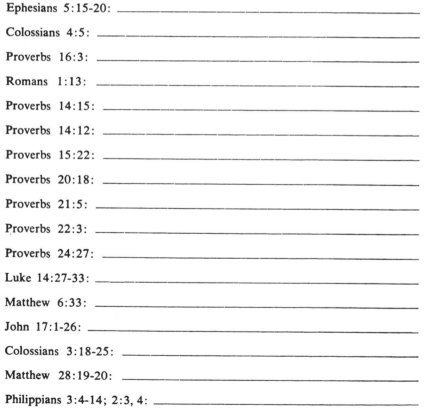

Ephesians 5:15-20: _____

Colossians 4:5: _____

Proverbs 16:3: _____

Romans 1:13: _____

Proverbs 14:15: _____

Proverbs 14:12: _____

Proverbs 15:22: _____

Proverbs 20:18: _____

Proverbs 21:5: _____

Proverbs 22:3: _____

Proverbs 24:27: _____

Luke 14:27-33: _____

Matthew 6:33: _____

John 17:1-26: _____

Colossians 3:18-25: _____

Matthew 28:19-20: _____

Philippians 3:4-14; 2:3, 4: _____

Study these verses and, after reading each, ask, "What do I learn about planning or use of time or priorities from this?" Write your thoughts down on a piece of paper and bring them with you for counseling.

B. Planning for Lordship

1. Evaluate how you spend your time. Use the form on pages 134-136 to get a picture of how you use your time. Fill this form out as a daily journal. Then ask what things on the daily journal get the most time. Are they the things God considers most important?

2. Make a list of things to be done in order of priority. Judge the importance of each according to God's values and not merely your own desires. Make sure you include all of your God-given responsibilities in every area. Think through your entire life—spiritual, social, emotional, family, physical, intellectual, occupational, church, Christian service, financial, home, etc.

3. Make up a schedule of a week which would honor Christ by providing adequate and balanced time for all those life priorities required in the Bible. Use the form provided on pages 137-138. Use this schedule flexibly as a basic guide for life.

4. Establish goals for your life in every area. Use the form provided on pages 139-144. Write out your goals in specific terms and plan a step-by-step approach to accomplish these goals. Make sure your goals are realistic and your plans are concrete and specific. To establish these goals and bring them to reality, make sure you write any possible obstacles you may encounter in fulfilling these goals and your solutions to these obstacles. Discuss these goals and plans with your counselor or a godly friend and ask for suggestions and criticism. Make these goals a matter of prayer, review them frequently, revamp them when necessary, and periodically evaluate your progress in fulfilling them. As certain goals are attained, establish other goals and press on. Here is one example of a goal you might adopt and some specific plans to bring it to fruition.

Spiritual Goal: To become a more mature disciple of Jesus Christ.

Plan: To spend 30 minutes each morning using a quiet-time guide.

To read at least one Christian book every month.

To memorize at least two verses of Scripture every week.

To ask my wife or a close Christian friend to check up on me in areas of weakness, to pray for me, to exhort me when I seem to be slipping.

Possible Obstacles: Difficult to get up on time.

Sometimes I don't wake up very quickly and may not profit from my devotions.

Cost of books is increasing.

Pride—I don't want to make myself vulnerable by exposing my weaknesses to another person.

Possible Solutions: Get to bed earlier the night before.

Get a good alarm clock.

133

Wash, shave, brush teeth, exercise before devotions to get me wide awake.
Borrow books from church library instead of buying; or arrange with
   friends to share books with each other—I with them and they with me.
Humble myself under the mighty hand of God; memorize verses on
   humility and the need to have the help of others. Repent of pride
   and do what I ought to do.

Ephesians 5:16

Keep a detailed record of how you use your time. Make a note of everything you
do and how much time you spend doing it (e.g., Monday—TV 2 hours; 1½ hours
eating; 1 hour devotions; 1 hour talking to mate; 30 minutes on telephone calls;
30 minutes writing letters; 30 minutes hygiene and dressing; 7½ hours sleeping;
30 minutes playing ping-pong, reading, etc).

Monday

1. _____   10. _____

2. _____   11. _____

3. _____   12. _____

4. _____   13. _____

5. _____   14. _____

6. _____   15. _____

7. _____   16. _____

8. _____   17. _____

9. _____   18. _____

Tuesday

1. _____   10. _____

2. _____   11. _____

3. _____   12. _____

4. _____   13. _____

5. _____   14. _____

6. _____   15. _____

7. _____   16. _____

8. _____   17. _____

9. _____   18. _____

Wednesday

1. _____	10. _____
2. _____	11. _____
3. _____	12. _____
4. _____	13. _____
5. _____	14. _____
6. _____	15. _____
7. _____	16. _____
8. _____	17. _____
9. _____	18. _____

Thursday

1. _____	10. _____
2. _____	11. _____
3. _____	12. _____
4. _____	13. _____
5. _____	14. _____
6. _____	15. _____
7. _____	16. _____
8. _____	17. _____
9. _____	18. _____

Friday

1. _____	11. _____
2. _____	12. _____
3. _____	13. _____
4. _____	14. _____
5. _____	15. _____
6. _____	16. _____
7. _____	17. _____
8. _____	18. _____
9. _____	19. _____
10. _____	20. _____

Saturday

1. _____   11. _____
2. _____   12. _____
3. _____   13. _____
4. _____   14. _____
5. _____   15. _____
6. _____   16. _____
7. _____   17. _____
8. _____   18. _____
9. _____   19. _____
10. _____   20. _____

Sunday

1. _____   11. _____
2. _____   12. _____
3. _____   13. _____
4. _____   14. _____
5. _____   15. _____
6. _____   16. _____
7. _____   17. _____
8. _____   18. _____
9. _____   19. _____
10. _____   20. _____

Structure

Prepare a Time Budget—Look over the items on your list of things you do and evaluate what you are doing. Then transfer these items to the appropriate list below.

1. Items to continue in your present schedule

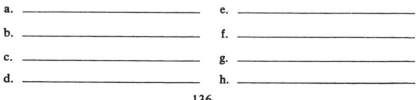

a. _____   e. _____
b. _____   f. _____
c. _____   g. _____
d. _____   h. _____

136

i. _____ p. _____

j. _____ q. _____

k. _____ r. _____

l. _____ s. _____

m. _____ t. _____

n. _____ u. _____

o. _____

2. Items on which to omit or decrease the time spent

a. _____ e. _____

b. _____ f. _____

c. _____ g. _____

d. _____ h. _____

3. Items on which to add time (e.g., family devotions, time alone with mate, etc.)

a. _____ g. _____

b. _____ h. _____

c. _____ i. _____

d. _____ j. _____

e. _____ k. _____

f. _____

SCHEDULE FOR WEEK OF _____ TODAY'S DATE _____

Time	Sunday	Monday	Tuesday	Wednesday	Thursday	Friday	Saturday
6							
7							
8							
8:30							
9							
10							

10:30							
11							
11:30							
12							
1							
1:30							
2							
2:30							
3							
3:30							
4							
4:30							
5							
5:30							
6							
6:30							
7							
7:30							
8							
9							
10							
10:30							
11							

Personal Goals

I. *Spiritual*
  A. Goals

     1. _____

     2. _____

     3. _____

     4. _____

  B. Possible Obstacles

     1. _____

     2. _____

     3. _____

     4. _____

  C. Possible Solutions

     1. _____

     2. _____

     3. _____

     4. _____

II. *Family*
  A. Goals

     1. _____

     2. _____

     3. _____

     4. _____

  B. Possible Obstacles

     1. _____

     2. _____

     3. _____

     4. _____

C. Possible Solutions

    1. _____

    2. _____

    3. _____

    4. _____

III. *Christian Service or Ministry*

A. Goals

    1. _____

    2. _____

    3. _____

    4. _____

B. Possible Obstacles

    1. _____

    2. _____

    3. _____

    4. _____

C. Possible Solutions

    1. _____

    2. _____

    3. _____

    4. _____

IV. *Social*

A. Goals

    1. _____

    2. _____

    3. _____

    4. _____

B. Possible Obstacles

    1. _____

2. _____

3. _____

4. _____

C. Possible Solutions

   1. _____

   2. _____

   3. _____

   4. _____

V. *Intellectual*

A. Goals

   1. _____

   2. _____

   3. _____

   4. _____

B. Possible Obstacles

   1. _____

   2. _____

   3. _____

   4. _____

C. Possible Solutions

   1. _____

   2. _____

   3. _____

   4. _____

VI. *Physical*

A. Goals

   1. _____

   2. _____

   3. _____

   4. _____

B. Possible Obstacles

    1. _____

    2. _____

    3. _____

    4. _____

C. Possible Solutions

    1. _____

    2. _____

    3. _____

    4. _____

VII. *Occupational*

A. Goals

    1. _____

    2. _____

    3. _____

    4. _____

B. Possible Obstacles

    1. _____

    2. _____

    3. _____

    4. _____

C. Possible Solutions

    1. _____

    2. _____

    3. _____

    4. _____

VIII. *Financial*

A. Goals

    1. _____

142

      2. _____

      3. _____

      4. _____

  B. Possible Obstacles

      1. _____

      2. _____

      3. _____

      4. _____

  C. Possible Solutions

      1. _____

      2. _____

      3. _____

      4. _____

IX. *Emotional*

  A. Goals

      1. _____

      2. _____

      3. _____

      4. _____

  B. Possible Obstacles

      1. _____

      2. _____

      3. _____

      4. _____

  C. Possible Solutions

      1. _____

      2. _____

      3. _____

      4. _____

PRIDE

Overcoming the Sin of Pride

A Bible study developed by Raymond Richards and Wayne A. Mack.

ORIGIN OF PRIDE

1. Study Genesis 3:1-6. In what specific way did Adam and Eve commit the

   sin of pride? _____

   _____

   What effect has sin had upon man's spiritual condition? Study these verses
   and write out your answer.

   Genesis 6:5: _____

   Jeremiah 17:9: _____

   Mark 7:21, 22: _____

   _____

   Romans 8:5-7: _____

   I Corinthians 2:15: _____

   Ephesians 2:3: _____

   Ephesians 4:17-19: _____

   Colossians 1:21: _____

   Titus 3:3: _____

   I Peter 4:2-4: _____

   _____

   John 3:19: _____

2. Before any person can have the ability to overcome any sin, especially the
   sin of pride, what must first take place in his life?

   Psalm 51:10: _____

   Isaiah 57:15: _____

Ezekiel 36:27: _____

John 3:3: _____

I Corinthians 2:12: _____

II Corinthians 5:17: _____

Jesus said, "Apart from me ye can do nothing" (John 15:5). Apart from being born again you cannot begin to overcome the deep-rooted sin of pride. Have you been born again? Has God imparted new life to you through the Holy Spirit? Have you repented of your sins, trusted in Christ as the only Saviour from your sins, and continued to obey Him as Lord?

_____

_____

3. List several reasons why you should be concerned about overcoming pride. Get out a Bible concordance and note the devastating effects of pride.

It is sin (Mark 7:22).   _____

It hinders frindships (Tit. 3:3).   _____

_____   _____

_____   _____

_____   _____

4. Study the following verses to discover the various ways pride is seen in men. Circle the verses which describe ways you manifest pride.

Genesis 11:4: _____

Exodus 5:2: _____

Judges 9:28, 29: _____

Psalm 10:4: _____

Psalm 12:3, 4: _____

Psalm 73:3-6: _____

Psalm 101:5: _____

Psalm 131:1: _____

Proverbs 13:10: _____

Proverbs 13:18: _____

145

Proverbs 25:6: _____

Proverbs 25:14: _____

Isaiah 3:16: _____

Jeremiah 48:29: _____

Jeremiah 45:5a: _____

Ezekiel 28:2: _____

Daniel 5:20: _____

Isaiah 14:13, 14: _____

Matthew 6:1-7: _____

_____

Mark 9:34: _____

I Corinthians 4:7: _____

I Corinthians 8:1: _____

Jude 16: _____

III John 9: _____

In what ways can God take your sinful words and actions, change your manner, and purify your attitudes and motives and use similar actions or words or questions in a positive, constructive, and God-honoring way? Example: Instead of pushing myself to do things I do not have the ability to do (Prov. 25:14), I will concentrate on doing the things that are within my grasp to the best of my ability, for the service of other people, and for the glory of God.

Review the Biblical examples which you circled that indicate your sinful attitudes and actions. How might God change your attitudes and motives and use your actions, words, and qualities for the good of others and His glory? On the spaces below, write out the specific plan you will use to put off the sinful practices and put on the new Biblical practices (Eph. 4:22-24).

Problem: Want public recognition (III John 9)

Solution: Unselfishly use my gifts and abilities to serve others.

1. Problem: _____

   Solution: _____

2. Problem: _____

   Solution: _____

146

3. Problem: _____

   Solution: _____

4. Problem: _____

   Solution: _____

Begin immediately to put the Biblical practices into action.

5. Read the following verses and note what happens to the proud man.

   Isaiah 2:17: _____

   Proverbs 16:18: _____

   Proverbs 18:12: _____

   Judges 9:38-41: _____

   I Peter 5:5: _____

   Galatians 6:3: _____

   Romans 12:3: _____

   Isaiah 2:15-23: _____

   _____

   I Timothy 6:3-5: _____

   Have you experienced the tragic consequences of pride? In what specific ways has your pride brought God's judgment upon your life, promoted an unrealistic estimation of yourself, or caused strife and contention in your relationships with other people?

   _____

   _____

   _____

   _____

6. Look up Proverbs 18:12 and note what character quality should replace pride in the Christian's life.

   _____

   How would you define humility? _____

   _____

7. The Lord Jesus Christ is the greatest example of humility. Jesus said, ". . .

147

take my yoke upon you and learn of me." It is the duty of every Christian to walk as Christ walked, to acquire the same attitudes and responses, goals and purposes as Jesus Christ. This is possible because the Holy Spirit dwells in every Christian, enabling him to become like Christ. Study the following passages and write down the specific ways Christ humbled Himself.

John 17:4: _____

John 5:30: _____

II Corinthians 8:9: _____

Matthew 20:28: _____

John 10:11: _____

Luke 2:16: _____

II Corinthians 5:21: _____

Philippians 2:6-8: _____

Galatians 4:4: _____

Isaiah 53:2, 3: _____

Isaiah 53:6, 7: _____

_____

Isaiah 53:10: _____

In short summary, write out the "rights" Jesus gave up in order to be our Savior and God's servant.

_____

_____

_____

_____

Are you more concerned about defending your personal rights than in fulfilling your responsibilities? Make a list of all the things you consider to be your "personal rights." Example: "I have worked harder than anyone else on this job! I deserve and have a right to a raise in salary!" After you have made your list, in a prayer give all your rights up to God. Review your list of rights daily and add to the list as others come to mind. As one who has been redeemed by the blood of Jesus Christ, you no longer have personal rights. You have been bought with a price; you are not your own. God may give your "rights" back as a privilege for which you can thank Him. The next time someone intrudes in an area you consider to be your personal rights, do not retaliate. Rather apply Matthew 5:38-48 and I Peter 2:23.

8. Jesus Christ was God, in every sense equal with the Father, yet He made Himself of no reputation. How does each of these following verses describe the posture or manner in which our Lord lived?

Isaiah 42:1: _____

Isaiah 52:13: _____

Philippians 2:7: _____

Matthew 20:28: _____

Study John 13:3-17 and note how Jesus Christ demonstrated that He was a servant and that all who follow Him must be servants.

_____

_____

Make a list of the ways you can use your time, resources, and abilities to serve God by serving your husband/wife, children, church, employee/employer, neighbors, etc. Do so because the Bible commands you to "let this mind dwell in you which is also in Christ Jesus" (Phil. 2:5), and not for the purpose of having others do good to you.

9. What does Paul warn against in Romans 12:3?

_____

According to Galatians 6:3, what is the result of having an inflated and un-realistic opinion of one's self?

_____

Make a list of all your abilities and plan how you will use them to serve others. After you have made your list, ask some godly Christian who knows you quite well to evaluate your list to see if it is an accurate assessment of your gifts, talents, and abilities.

10. What promises does God make to those who humble themselves?

Proverbs 18:12: _____

Proverbs 15:33: _____

Matthew 23:12: _____

James 4:10: _____

I Peter 5:5: _____

What do you think it means to "humble yourself under the mighty hand of

God"? _____

_____

11. How does God bless and exalt those who humbly accept and fulfill their present responsibilities and manifest the fruit of the Spirit?

Genesis 39:1-6: _____

_____

Job 22:29: _____

Job 42:1-17: _____

_____

Psalm 113:7, 8: _____

Psalm 147:3: _____

Psalm 34:18: _____

Luke 15:11-24: _____

_____

_____

Study Matthew 25:14-30. What did the two faithful servants have in common?

_____

In what specific way did the master "exalt" the two faithful servants?

_____

What did the unfaithful servant fail to do? (vs. 27) _____

_____

Why did he refuse to invest the money given to him? _____

_____

What was the final outcome of his unfaithfulness and selfishness? (vss. 28-30)

_____

_____

Matthew 25:31-46. What is the scene being described? _____

_____

In what specific manner did Christ contrast the humble with the proud, the sheep with the goats? _____

_____

What reward did Jesus promise to those who out of love for Him demonstrate their love by unselfish acts of giving to those in need? (vss. 34, 46)

_____

What will be the penalty for those whose selfishness and self-centeredness reflect that they have not been rightly related to God through Jesus Christ?

(vss. 41, 46) _____

_____

With whom did the righteous identify themselves? (vs. 40) _____

_____

What will be the final home and continual joy of those whom Christ will

exalt? (Rev. 5:9-12) _____

_____

List some of the personal insights, challenges, convictions, and blessings you received from this study.

_____

_____

_____

_____

_____

_____

PROBLEM SOLVING

Problem Solution Sheet

When a problem arises, sit down and evaluate the problem in the following manner.
A. First, discern the different levels of the problem.
   1. What were your feelings before, during, and after the problem arose?
   2. What were you doing or what happened when the problem arose? If some-
      one else was involved, what did he/she do? Did you do or say anything in
      the past or present that may have helped to precipitate the problem? Were
      there things you didn't do that may have precipitated the problem? What
      wrong actions were involved in the problem? What responsibilities have
      you been neglecting?
   3. *What wrong attitudes may be associated with the problem?* Where does
      your thinking need to be corrected? Do you have beliefs or attitudes that
      are aggravating the problem? Are the beliefs or attitudes you have about
      the problem Biblical?
   4. Is this the first time you have ever had this problem? If not, with whom
      did you have the problem? What happened? What did you do? How did
      you react? Was the problem solved? What was the outcome?
B. Second, discover the Biblical way of handling this problem.
   1. What does God want you to do about this problem? Search the Scriptures
      to find God's solution. Ask God to give you wisdom in understanding and
      knowing how to apply His Word.
   2. Write down the specific things you should do to solve the problem God's
      way.
   3. If you can't find God's solution by yourself, write down what is keeping
      you from finding it and ask your counselor to help you.
C. Third, specifically confess to God what you have been doing wrong and de-
   cisively commit yourself to do what is right.
   1. Verbalize your confession and commitment to God in prayer. Ask God for
      help to obey and trust Him to give it.
   2. It might also be helpful to write out your commitment on a piece of paper
      and then sign the paper. This will make your commitment very real and
      binding.
   3. If your wrong actions or way of handling a problem have involved or hurt
      another person, you ought to ask that person for forgiveness.
   4. It may also be helpful to share your commitment to Biblical action with
      someone else and ask him/her to help you keep your commitment.
D. Fourth, discipline yourself and actually put the Biblical course of action into
   practice.

1. Deliberately and resolutely begin to do what the Bible tells you to do. Do what you ought to do regardless of how you feel.
2. Structure your life for change.
   a. Wherever possible, eliminate those things that encourage unbiblical action or thinking.
   b. Add or continue those things that encourage Biblical action and thinking.
3. Exercise immediate restraint at the point of temptation (Prov. 17:14; James 4:7).
4. Ask some godly person or persons to help you overcome your problem (Heb. 10:24, 25; Gal. 6:1, 2).
5. Commune with Christ your Saviour and Lord by prayer, Bible study, meditation, and involvement in the worship services of a church where the Bible is believed and preached (John 15:1-6; II Tim. 3:16, 17; Heb. 10:24, 25; Isa. 40:31; James 5:16-18).
6. Practice the new pattern of action consistently and constantly (I Tim. 4:7; Heb. 5:14; Luke 9:23).

READING ASSIGNMENT QUESTIONNAIRE

Read _____

A. Write down the most important principles or insights presented by the author in this booklet.

B. Do you agree or disagree with the author? Put a check mark where you disagree. If you disagree, give your reasons.

C. Evaluate or assess your life in the light of the insights presented in this booklet. Note where you are failing and where you are succeeding in implementing the truths of this booklet. What do you need to change? How will you go about making the changes?

READING MATERIAL USED AS COUNSELING HOMEWORK

This list is only suggestive, not exhaustive.

Pamphlets or books by Jay E. Adams on—
Christ and Your Problems, Fear, Worry, Depression, Anger, Hooked (alcohol and drugs), A Personal Word to Women, Godliness Through Discipline (published by Presbyterian and Reformed Publishing Co., and available from Christian Study Services, 1790 East Willow Grove Avenue, Laverock, Pa. 19118).

Devotional booklet designed to help counselors implement Biblical change, by Jay E. Adams, *Four Weeks with God and Your Neighbor* (available from Christian Study Services).

Book by Jay E. Adams, *How to Overcome Evil* (available from Christian Study Services).

Books and booklets by Wayne A. Mack—
The Bible's Answer to the Question, What Is a Christian? (Mack Publishing Co.).
Profitable Bible Reading (Presbyterian and Reformed).
How to Pray Effectually (Presbyterian and Reformed).
How to Develop Deep Unity in the Marriage Relationship (Presbyterian and Reformed).
The Biblical Concept of Church Discipline (Mack Publishing Co.).
(These books and booklets may be purchased from Mrs. Carol Mack, 511 Fisher Lane, Warminster, PA 18974.)

Articles from various volumes of *The Journal of Pastoral Practice* (available from Christian Study Services)—

Volume I, Number 1
Counseling Decision Makers, Howard Eyrich and Bruce Strickland
Illness and a Life View, Robert Smith, M.D.
A Physician Looks at Depression, Robert Smith, M.D.
A Physician Looks at Symptoms, Robert Smith, M.D.

Volume I, Number 2
When the Children Leave Home, Wayne A. Mack
What in the Church Is a Woman to Do? Paul Settle
A look at Psychosomatic Relationships, Robert Smith, M.D.

Volume II, Number 1
Indicators of Learning Disability, James E. Alpaugh
Biblical Help for Solving Interpersonal Conflicts, Wayne A. Mack
Yourself and You, Larry S. Ruddell
Your Good Health, Robert Smith, M.D.
Health Books, Robert Smith, M.D.

Volume II, Number 2
Biblical Help for Overcoming Depression, Wayne A. Mack

Chapters from book by James Montgomery Boice, *How to Really Live It Up* (Zondervan Publishing House; available from Christian Study Services)

Christian Financial Concepts, Larry Burkett (published by Christian Financial Concepts)

Joni, Joni Eareckson (Zondervan)

Not by Accident, Isabel Fleece (Moody Press)

You Can Be Financially Free, George Fooshee, Jr. (Revell Co.; available from Christian Study Services)

The Christian Looks at Himself, Anthony A. Hoekema (Eerdmans; available from Christian Study Services)

Quiet Time (InterVarsity Press)

What the Scriptures Teach, Ernest Kevan (Evangelical Press, P.O. Box 2453, Grand Rapids)

The Bible Tells Us So, R. B. Kuiper (Banner of Truth Trust)

Single and Human, Ada Lum (InterVarsity Press)

Members One of Another, Eric Lane (Evangelical Press)

Spiritual Depression, Its Causes and Cure, Martin Lloyd Jones (Eerdmans)

The Bible and Drug Abuse, Robert Morey (Presbyterian and Reformed)

None of These Diseases, S. I. McMillen, M.D. (Revell Co.)

Defeating Despair and Depression, Matilda Nortveilt (Moody Press; available from Christian Study Services)

Chapters from a book entitled *The Way,* Godfrey Robinson and Stephen Winward (Moody Press)

Booklets by J. C. Ryle entitled *Sickness* and *Never Perish* (Evangelical Press)

Chapters from *No Little People,* Francis Schaeffer (InterVarsity Press)

Hidden Art, Edith Schaeffer (Tyndale House)

Living and Loving, A. N. Truton (InterVarsity Press)

Chapters from *Knowing God,* J. I. Packer (InterVarsity Press)

Comfort for Christians, A. W. Pink (Reiner Publications, Swengel, PA)

A catalog listing additional books and booklets helpful for Biblical counseling may be secured from Christian Study Services, 1790 E. Willow Grove Avenue, Laverock, PA 19118.

SELF-CONTROL
(Discipline)

Study the following verses and note everything they have to say about self-control or discipline. Write down what they say about: the lack of self-control—its results; the importance of self-control; the different areas in which we need self-control (e.g., words, thoughts, etc.); the method or means by which we attain self-control; the results of self-control; the blessings of self-control; and the dangers or harm of lacking self-control. Choose several verses to memorize and begin. Note the areas in which you have the greatest trouble and devise a specific plan of action for improving these areas. (Look at the NASB Version as you do this study.)

I Timothy 4:7: _____

II Timothy 1:7; 2:1-7, 15: _____

I Corinthians 9:24-27: _____

I Thessalonians 4:11, 12; 5:14: _____

II Thessalonians 3:6-15: _____

I Peter 1:13: _____

Philippians 4:8: _____

James 3:4-8: _____

Ephesians 5:16: _____

Galatians 5:22, 23: _____

Proverbs 23:1-3; 25:16: _____

Romans 13:14: _____

I Thessalonians 5:6-8: _____

II Peter 1:3-8: _____

Hebrews 5:14: _____

Proverbs 4:20-27: _____

Luke 9:23-24: _____

Hebrews 12:11: _____

Acts 24:16: _____

Proverbs 12:1: _____

Proverbs 13:1: _____

Proverbs 13:3, 18, 24: _____

Proverbs 14:29: _____

Proverbs 15:5, 10, 31, 32: _____

Proverbs 16:32: _____

Proverbs 17:27, 28: _____

Proverbs 19:16, 18, 20: _____

Proverbs 19:27: _____

Proverbs 20:3, 13, 25: _____

Proverbs 19:2: _____

Proverbs 20:5: _____

Proverbs 21:21, 23: _____

Proverbs 22:15, 17, 18, 24, 25: _____

Proverbs 23:12, 13, 14, 19: _____

Proverbs 23:29, 30: _____

Proverbs 24:27, 30-34: _____

Proverbs 25:8, 17, 27, 28: _____

Proverbs 28:20: _____

Proverbs 29:11, 20, 22: _____

Proverbs 30:32, 33: _____

Psalm 57:7: _____

Philippians 2:5-8: _____

SELF-LOVE

Study the following verses and note everything they have to say about self-love. Answer questions from these verses, such as—Does the Bible encourage us to work directly on our self-image? What does the Bible suggest about self-love? Focusing on self? Are people down on themselves sometimes for good reasons? What is to be the focus or center of a Christian's thoughts? Write out your answers and note ways in which you need to change.

Mark 12:29-31: _____

James 2:8; 1:26; 4:9, 10: _____

Leviticus 19:18: _____

Ephesians 5:28, 29; 2:19: _____

Mark 10:39: _____

Matthew 16:24, 25: _____

Ephesians 4:22-24; 2:19: _____

Romans 6:6; 12:1; 6:11; 1:11, 12; 15:24: _____

_____

Romans 2:8, 9; 12:16, 3; 8:32: _____

_____

Philippians 2:20, 21: _____

I Corinthians 13:4, 5: _____

Proverbs 3:5, 6; 14:12; 16:24: _____

_____

II Corinthians 1:9: _____

I John 3:19, 20: _____

Colossians 2:10; 3:4, 10: _____

I Peter 2:9: _____

I Thessalonians 5:5; 2:8: _____

Philippians 4:13, 19, 16; 2:3, 4: _____

_____

Daniel 10:11, 12: _____

I Corinthians 10:13: _____

Hebrews 10:24, 25: _____

Acts 20:35: _____

SERVICE

Christian Service Involvement

Name ———————————————

Date ———————————————

Nature of Service	If Involved	Specify Approximate Hours per Month
1. Bible studies		
2. Visitation		
3. Tape ministry		
4. Sunday School		
5. Youth work		
6. Nursing homes		
7. Tract distribution		
8. Music		
9. Book room		
10. Office work		
11. Street meetings		
12. Bible clubs		
13. Park services		
14. Works of mercy		
15. Hospitality		
16. Buildings and grounds		
17. Transportation		
18. Counseling		
19. College age		

20. Helping people in practical ways _____

21. Children's work _____

22. Reading or helping the sick and aged _____

23. Baby or child sitting _____

24. Dispensing or delivering tapes locally _____

25. Forming and operating a tape
listening group _____

26. Discipling others _____

27. Administrative work _____

28. Writing _____

29. Tutoring _____

30. Publications _____

31. Publicity _____

32. Using telephone for Christ,
announcements, prayer requests _____

33. Receptionist _____

34. Ushering _____

35. Canvassing or surveying for Christ _____

36. Correspondence _____

37. Nursery _____

38. Adult fellowship _____

39. Men's meetings _____

40. Women's meetings _____

41. Committee or board meetings _____

42. Evangelism _____

43. Daily Vacation Bible School _____

44. Cleaning for needy people _____

45. Cooking for needy people _____

46. Sewing for needy people _____

47. Purchasing supplies _____

48. Mailing _____

49. Mimeograph work _____

50. Printing _____

51. Carpentry or other practical work
    in the name of Christ _____

SEX PROBLEMS

ASSIGNMENT FOR WEEK _____

1. Study—

Leviticus 18:22: _____

Romans 1:24-32: _____

I Corinthians 6:9-11: _____

I Timothy 1:8-11: _____

II Timothy 2:22: _____

Matthew 5:27-32: _____

Jude 7, 8: _____

II Corinthians 10:4, 5: _____

Leviticus 20:13: _____

Genesis 19:1-29: _____

I Corinthians 9:24-27: _____

Galatians 5:24: _____

Romans 8:32, 37: _____

I Corinthians 10:13: _____

Romans 13:11-14: _____

Romans 6:1-23: _____

Proverbs 7:1-27: _____

Proverbs 5:20-25: _____

Proverbs 13:20: _____

Proverbs 17:14: _____

Proverbs 18:10: _____

Proverbs 19:3: _____

Proverbs 22:3: _____

Proverbs 22:24, 25: _____

Proverbs 23:20, 21: _____

Proverbs 23:26, 27, 28: _____

Proverbs 26:20-22: _____

Proverbs 29:3: _____

Proverbs 29:18: _____

Proverbs 27:17, 12: _____

Psalm 119:9-11: _____

Acts 20:32: _____

Romans 12:1-2: _____

Ephesians 4:7-16: _____

Genesis 39:1-12: _____

Write down everything that these passages have to say about sexual immorality. Note also in detailed fashion what these passages tell you about overcoming sexual immorality. Apply it to your situation and make a list of specific things you should do and steps you should take. Put your plan into action immediately and daily.

2. Keep a *daily journal* of *when* you are tempted, *where* you are, *with whom* you are, *what* is happening, what you were *thinking* about and *doing before* and *during* the temptation, *what you do* when you are tempted and *after* the temptation.

3. Choose several verses out of those listed and begin to memorize them. Review them daily.

SLEEP

A. Possible Effects of Sleep Loss
1. Tiredness, fatigue, weariness.
2. Emotional-irritability, suspiciousness, easily discouraged, depression, problems seem enlarged, etc.
3. May see things, hear things, feel things that aren't there—hallucinations.
4. Difficulty concentrating, thinking, studying, remembering, etc.
5. Injury to the body.
Evaluate the effects that your sleep loss has on you. Circle the words which apply to you.

B. Possible Contributing Causes of Sleep Loss
1. Bad scheduling—irregularity in bedtime.
2. Organic problems—arthritis, hypothyroid conditions, etc.
3. Shift work.
4. Bad habits—late TV programs, wasting time during day, napping during day, eating before bedtime, drinking too much coffee or other stimulants during day or before bedtime, diet pills or other drugs.
5. Lack of exercise or activity (Eccles. 5:12).
6. Worry, grief, bitterness, resentment, anger, guilt, fear, etc.
7. Planning or thinking or other activities at bedtime that stimulate rather than relax.
8. Bringing work or too much excitement into the bedroom.
Circle the words or phrases which may contribute to your sleep loss. Add any other items that you think may contribute to your problem.

C. Overcoming Sleep Loss
1. Prayer. Write down what the following verses say about sleep. Proverbs 3:13-24; Psalm 127:2; Psalm 4:8. Ask God to help you sleep, commit your problems into God's care, picture yourself turning your cares one by one over to God. Praise and thank God for Himself and His many blessings.
2. Confess your sins to God on a daily basis. Don't rationalize, deny, or excuse your sins. (Study Ps. 32:1-7; Prov. 28:13; I John 1:9.)
3. If you are physically able, do something physical—work or exercise—to the point of perspiration on a regular basis (Eccles. 5:12; Prov. 14:23).
4. Take a hot shower or warm bath before retiring.
5. Drink warm milk before retiring.
6. Make sure you have a comfortable mattress.
7. Have a night pad beside your bed on which you may write the ideas or problems that come into your mind when you retire. Put them on paper and resolve to leave them there until tomorrow morning.

8. Avoid stimulants of any kind (coffee, tea, soft drinks, etc.) before retiring. Perhaps you ought to eliminate them entirely. It's worth a try.

9. Avoid eating after your evening meal (don't eat your evening meal too close to bedtime). Sometimes it helps to eat your bigger meal at noon and your lighter meal in the evening.

10. Make your bedroom a sleep room, not a work room or play room.

11. Avoid watching TV programs that tend to alarm, distress, or excite you before bedtime.

12. Deal with your problems during the day, so you won't have to worry or fret or feel guilty about them when you go to bed at night.

13. Avoid taking naps during the day.

14. Do some relaxation exercises before you retire. It's especially important to have the neck muscles relaxed when you go to bed. Sometimes wrapping your pillow around the back of the neck will help.

15. Married people often find sexual relations to the point of orgasm helpful in getting to sleep.

16. Establish a pattern of regularity in your sleep habits. Go to bed at the same time and get up at the same time. God created us with a capacity to learn habits and patterns.

17. Some people find that relaxing music helps them to get to sleep.

18. Meditate on God's promises, His goodness, His blessings, His comfort, His mercies, His assurances, His protection, His power, His faithfulness, etc. Reflect on favorite and comforting passages of Scripture such as Romans 8:16-39; Psalm 23; Psalm 27:1-4. This is not a time for memorizing, but it is a time to enjoy what you have already memorized. Practice Philippians 4:8, and you will soon be asleep or else you won't care if you don't because you will be enjoying yourself so much.

19. Recognize the fact that an occasional night when you have difficulty sleeping or getting asleep or staying asleep is quite common and will not seriously harm you unless you let it. Don't focus on or worry about not getting to sleep. Instead, follow the suggestions made in this study and you'll probably be asleep in a short time. If you are afraid you won't go to sleep and worry about it, you probably won't. Your fear will produce the thing you fear. Remember also that on rare occasions God may withhold sleep because He wants you to spend extra time in prayer or meditation (Luke 6:12; II Cor. 11:27). On these rare (and I am sure they are intended to be rare) occasions, relax and make the best use of your time.

20. Keep a daily journal of your problems, conflicts, fears, worries, anger, or resentment. To help you sleep properly we may have to help you deal with those matters in a Biblical way.

21. Keep a daily journal of:
    a. The time you go to bed.
    b. What you think about or do before and when you go to bed.
    c. What time you wake up.

STRUCTURING YOUR LIFE FOR BIBLICAL CHANGE

Name _____

Desired Change _____

A. Events, activities, associations, practices, etc., that need to be eliminated or decreased because they may encourage sinful attitudes and actions and make it difficult to change (Prov. 22:24, 25; 13:20; 14:7; I Cor. 15:33; Ps. 1:1; Rom. 13:11-14).

   1. _____

   2. _____

   3. _____

   4. _____

   5. _____

   6. _____

   7. _____

   8. _____

   9. _____

  10. _____

  11. _____

  12. _____

B. Events, activities, associations, practices, etc., that need to be added or increased because they encourage the right kind of thinking and acting (Ps. 119: 9, 11; Prov. 13:20; Josh. 1:8; Ps. 1:1-3; Ps. 101:3; Job 31:1; Heb. 10:24, 25; Heb. 12:2; Rom. 13:14).

   1. _____

   2. _____

   3. _____

4. _____

5. _____

6. _____

7. _____

8. _____

9. _____

10. _____

11. _____

12. _____

SUFFERING

Study the following verses and write down everything they have to say about suffering. This study is laid out for a six-day period between counseling sessions. Every day as you study, write down your answers to such questions as:
What is suffering?
What are the different kinds of suffering?
What are several reasons for suffering?
Are there benefits that may come from suffering? If so, what are they?
What are some of the dangers that we face when we suffer?
How should Christians regard suffering?
What promises does God give to His people who suffer?
What should Christians do as they face suffering?
How should Christians act during times of suffering?
Evaluate your attitude toward and your response to suffering in the light of what these Scriptures indicate. Specifically note how you should change to become more Biblical in your way of facing suffering.

Day 1

Acts 9:16: _____

Romans 8:17-26: _____

I Corinthians 4:12: _____

II Corinthians 1:3-11: _____

II Corinthians 2:1-8: _____

II Corinthians 4:7-18: _____

II Corinthians 6:3-10: _____

II Corinthians 7:5-7: _____

II Corinthians 11:23-29: _____

II Corinthians 12:7-11: _____

Day 2

Galatians 4:19, 20: _____

Philippians 1:12-30: _____

Philippians 3:20, 21: _____

Philippians 4:12-15: _____

Colossians 1:24: _____

I Thessalonians 1:6: _____

I Thessalonians 1:7, 8: _____

II Timothy 1:8-14: _____

II Timothy 2:8-13: _____

II Timothy 3:10-17: _____

Day 3

Hebrews 10:31-36: _____

Hebrews 12:1-11: _____

James 1:2-5, 12: _____

James 5:7-11: _____

I Peter 2:18-25: _____

I Peter 3:13-18: _____

I Peter 4:12-16: _____

I Peter 5:8-10: _____

Day 4

Genesis 3:16, 17: _____

Psalm 32:3-5: _____

Proverbs 13:12: _____

Proverbs 15:15: _____

Proverbs 17:22: _____

Proverbs 18:14: _____

Psalm 94:12: _____

Proverbs 3:11, 12: _____

Isaiah 19:19-22: _____

Day 5

Romans 5:3, 4: _____

Genesis 22:12-18: _____

Genesis 32:9-31: _____

Numbers 21:6, 7: _____

Judges 10:6-10: _____

II Chronicles 33:12, 13: _____

Psalm 18:5: _____

Psalm 119:67, 71: _____

Psalm 9:9: _____

Psalm 23:1-6: _____

Psalm 27:5, 6: _____

Psalm 46:1: _____

Psalm 50:15: _____

Day 6

Psalm 119:50, 52, 143: _____

Psalm 140:12: _____

Isaiah 41:10: _____

Isaiah 40:29-31: _____

Isaiah 42:3: _____

Matthew 5:4, 10-12: _____

Matthew 11:28: _____

John 14:1, 16, 18, 27: _____

Romans 15:14: _____

John 9:1-3: _____

John 11:1-4: _____

John 15:1-3: _____

II Thessalonians 1:3, 4: _____

172

TAPE LISTENING ASSIGNMENT QUESTIONNAIRE

Listen to tape entitled: _____

1. Write down the most important insights and principles presented by the speaker in this tape.

   _____

   _____

   _____

   _____

   _____

   _____

   _____

2. Do you agree or disagree with the speaker? Write out any opinion you would like to express about the content of the tape: I agree or disagree with the speaker because—

   _____

   _____

   _____

   _____

   _____

   _____

3. Evaluate or assess your life in light of the insights presented in this tape. Note where you are failing and where you are succeeding in implementing the truths of this tape. What do you need to change? How will you go about making the changes?

   _____

   _____

   _____

   _____

   _____

   _____

TAPES USED AS COUNSELING ASSIGNMENTS

The following list includes tapes that may be used to help people with various problems. They may be given out with the tape listening questionnaire. I usually tell people to listen to the tapes at least two times during the week and then respond to them. These tapes may be ordered for $3.00 each plus postage from Strengthening Ministries International, 4067 Waterford Drive, Center Valley, Pa. 18034.

Cassettes Available

Set 1.	Marriage and the Christian Home		$54.00
(18 Tapes)	God's Blueprint for Marriage	— 1 study	
	Role of the Husband	— 3 studies	
	Role of the Wife	— 2 studies	
	Solving Conflicts in Marriage	— 1 study	
	Communication in the Home	— 4 studies	
	Money	— 1 study	
	Sex	— 1 study	
	Children	— 6 studies	

Set 2.　Marriage and the Christian Home　$36.00
(12 Tapes)　(Does not include tapes on raising children)

Set 3.　Marriage and the Christian Home　$18.00
(6 Tapes)　(Tapes on raising children)

Set 4.　Christian Home Series　$18.00
(6 Tapes)　Leave — Cleave — Weave
　　Achieving Unity in Marriage
　　Role of the Husband
　　Role of the Wife
　　Children—2 Tapes

Set 5.　A Biblical Approach to Problem Solving—2 Tapes　$18.00
(6 Tapes)　The Constructive Use of Anger
　　The Peculiar Problems and Blessings of Old Age
　　Biblical Counseling
　　How to Handle Stress

Set 6.　You Can Be Adequate: Resources for Change　$18.00
(6 Tapes)　You Can Be Reunited: Healing Fractured Relationships
　　You Can Be Joyful: Overcoming Depression
　　You Can Be Nice: Overcoming Irritability and Impatience
　　You Can Be Contented: Overcoming Discontentment
　　　and Inferiority

Set 7.	Knowing the Will of God—3 Tapes	
(6 Tapes)	Spiritual Gifts—3 Tapes	
Set 8.	Evangelistic Album — How to Be Gloriously Free;	$18.00
(6 Tapes)	Who Will Enter the Kingdom of Heaven; He Shall	
	Save; Rest for Your Soul; Jesus and Your Sin	
	Problem; Trust and Obey	
Set 9.	The Christian's Resources for Change	$18.00
(6 Tapes)	How to Build Up Your Faith	
	How to Be an Overcomer	
	How to Have a Life of Constant Fulness—2 Tapes	
	How to Find Real Joy	
Set 10.	Developing True Gratitude	$18.00
(6 Tapes)	Using Your Resources to Honor God	
	Developing an Effective Prayer Life	
	How to Overcome Boredom	
	What to Do When God Seems Far Away	
	How to Solve Your Identity Crisis	
Set 11.	The Biblical Ministry of Visitation	$18.00
(6 Tapes)	How to Face and Solve Problems in Your Life	
	The Role of Women in the Church—2 Tapes	
	How to Become an Effective Soulwinner	
	What God Wants the Church Member to Be	

CHANGING SINFUL THOUGHT PATTERNS

This study is designed to help you overcome the problem of sinful, destructive, God-dishonoring thought patterns. Sinful thought patterns include excessive suspiciousness; constant pessimism and negativism; envy; a critical, condemnatory, accusatory, judgmental attitude; bitterness; resentment; impulsiveness; vain regrets (looking to the past in such a way that it keeps you from living Biblically, responsibly, productively in the present); brooding, fretting; jumping to hasty and unfounded conclusions; daydreaming (inventing your own fantasy world, refusing to acknowledge faults, failures, reality); self-pity; wicked, immoral imaginations; etc.

1. Circle the phrase or phrases in the preceding paragraph and in the following paragraph that best describe the sinful thought patterns which you tend to have. I . . . often jump to conclusions; think others are talking about me behind my back; assume others are out to trap me; watch for the mistakes of others and am glad when I see them fail; don't listen to both sides of the story; tend to dwell on the other person's bad qualities; am quick to assume that other persons are wrong; often think the worst; exaggerate my problems or successes; exaggerate the faults and mistakes of others; often wish I was someone else or that I was some place else; often feel sorry for myself; I often don't see the sense in trying to change or improve; I often think about how others don't like me, don't appreciate me; I often reflect on how others have abused me or mistreated me; I frequently think about how much better off others are; etc.

   Be very objective and honest in evaluating your sinful thought patterns or you will not receive the help that this present study can provide for improvement. Remember, you probably will not be helped much unless you are aware of the specific ways in which you need assistance and change. Compare Proverbs 28:13.

2. For the next week (or until your next counseling session) keep a daily journal of your sinful thought patterns. On a daily basis write down every time you think in one of the ways you previously circled. Briefly record what happened, where you were, when it happend, with whom you were, and what you did when you became aware that you were thinking this way. Evaluate the way you handled this propensity in the light of what God wants you to do with such thoughts.

3. Read I Samuel 16:14-23. What was King Saul's attitude toward David?

   _____

   In what specific way did Saul honor David? (I Sam. 18:5) _____

   _____

4. Read I Samuel 18:6-9. How did Saul's attitude toward David change?

_____

According to I Samuel 18:8, what particular sin was at the root of Saul's problem? _____

Observe the different reactions Saul had to David's harp playing.

I Samuel 16:18: _____

I Samuel 18:10, 11: _____

Was the problem David's fault or Saul's fault? _____

_____

Did Saul have any basis for considering David a threat? Were Saul's suspicions well grounded? _____

5. What positive qualities that David possessed should Saul have dwelt upon and appreciated?

I Samuel 16:18: _____

I Samuel 17:32: _____

I Samuel 18:15: _____

I Samuel 18:16: _____

I Samuel 24:5, 6, 12: _____

I Samuel 26:11: _____

I Samuel 17:44-46: _____

6. Is there one particular person of whom you are especially suspicious, jealous, critical, judgmental? _____

Assignment No. 1:

In applying Philippians 4:8, make a list of 20 things you appreciate about that person. The list may include character qualities, attitudes, past deeds, gifts, talents, etc.

Examples:

I appreciate _____ because he/she is always consistent in church attendance.

I appreciate _____ because he/she keeps his/her bedroom tidy.

177

I appreciate _____ because he/she greets me and others warmly.

I appreciate my husband because he makes it part of his schedule to spend time with me and the children.

I appreciate my wife because she does her household duties regularly and faithfully without grumbling and complaining.

After you have made your "Appreciation List," thank God for the good qualities and actions displayed in his/her life and then seek opportunity to express your appreciation verbally to him/her. Keep a daily record of the times you express appreciation to people.

7. Study the following verses to discover what we shouldn't think and what we should think in reference to others. Write out in your own words what the verses mean.

Matthew 7:1-5: _____

_____

I Corinthians 13:5: _____

_____

Ephesians 4:31: _____

Ephesians 4:32: _____

Proverbs 19:11: _____

Proverbs 17:9: _____

Philippians 4:8: _____

Proverbs 12:25: _____

Proverbs 15:23: _____

Isaiah 50:4: _____

Proverbs 29:11: _____

Romans 12:17: _____

Romans 12:19-21: _____

_____

II Corinthians 10:5: _____

Genesis 6:5: _____

Philippians 1:3: _____

I Thessalonians 1:2: _____

Philippians 4:1: _____

Romans 1:8, 9: _____

II Corinthians 7:16: _____

Romans 16:1: _____

Romans 16:3, 4: _____

Philippians 2:22: _____

Philippians 2:25, 30: _____

II Corinthians 12:15: _____

8. The Bible has much to say about jumping to conclusions and how to handle a situation in which you actually have been offended. Look up these passages and write out what these verses mean to you.

Rash Judgment

Proverbs 18:2: _____

Proverbs 18:13: _____

Proverbs 18:17: _____

Proverbs 20:6: _____

Proverbs 25:8: _____

Proverbs 17:14: _____

Proverbs 14:15: _____

Proverbs 22:3: _____

Proverbs 29:11: _____

Proverbs 25:2: _____

Proverbs 16:20: _____

Proverbs 20:19: _____

Proverbs 26:20: _____

Proverbs 26:21: _____

Philippians 1:9, 10: _____

I Corinthians 13:7: _____

Reconciliation

Proverbs 26:9, 10: _____

Matthew 18:15: _____

Matthew 5:23. 24: _____

Luke 17:3, 4: _____

Matthew 6:14, 15: _____

Ephesians 4:32: _____

Assignment No. 2:

The Bible says, "Speak evil of no man" (Tit. 3:2). If you have jumped to conclusions about someone's activities, and your accusations have been made public and jeopardized another person's reputation, confess your sins to God and ask for His forgiveness. Then apply Matthew 5:23, 24 and confess your sins to the offended party and seek his/her forgiveness. Then go to all those with whom you have gossiped and confess your sin.

Write down several of the verses under "Rash Judgment" on a 3x5 index card. Every time you are tempted to impulsively condemn someone else or offer a rash opinion, read the verses on the card. Continue to do so until your sinful thinking pattern has been broken and replaced by the Biblical pattern. Carry the card with you at all times and review the verses continually. Force yourself to read or quote them whenever you are tempted to think or speak wrongly about another person. Ask God to help you to follow His directives and then proceed to do and think Biblically.

9. Read I Samuel 13:5-14; 15:1-31. What sinful pattern did Saul develop in his life which ultimately led to God's rejection of him as king of Israel?

(Refer particularly to 13:13; 15:11, 19, 23, 24) _____

_____

10. Study Proverbs 28:1. How does a guilty person act? _____

_____

11. What sins have you committed which you have failed to overcome and that have promoted a suspicious attitude?

a. _____

b. _____

c. _____

d. _____

e. _____

Assignment No. 3:

Confess those sins to God and ask for His forgiveness and then seek forgiveness from those persons whom you have sinned against. Ask someone who is close to you to covenant with you to help you overcome your sinful habits.

12. What bizarre behavior did Saul's suspicious, jealous, and rebellious attitude produce?

a. I Samuel 18:25: _____

b. I Samuel 19:1: _____

c. I Samuel 19:11: _____

d. I Samuel 20:33: _____

e. I Samuel 31:4: _____

13. What important fact was Saul unwilling to accept as final, true, and unchangeable? (I Sam. 15:28-30; 28:16-17).

_____

14. Has God providentially changed, removed, brought into, or taken from your life something you have been unwilling to accept which has promoted daydreaming, living in the past, or constructing a make-believe world in order to escape from your discontentment and dissatisfaction?

Examples:

I am unwilling to acknowledge that I am physically disabled.
I am unwilling to accept the fact that I have moved to another location, house, occupation.
I am unwilling to accept the fact that my husband/wife has passed away.
I am unwilling to acknowledge that I am getting older and cannot do some of the things I once could do.

_____

_____

_____

15. These verses address particularly the necessity of putting off false, wishful, imaginative, preoccupied, daydream thinking, and putting on the habit of thinking realistically, thankfully, unselfishly.

I Thessalonians 5:18: _____

Ephesians 5:20: _____

Philippians 4:4: _____

Psalm 34:1: _____

Deuteronomy 11:16: _____

Ecclesiastes 5:7: _____

Ecclesiastes 7:10: _____

II Timothy 1:7: _____

Philippians 1:9, 10: _____

Philippians 4:8: _____

Philippians 2:5-8: _____

Assignment No. 4:

List at least 30 things for which you should presently thank God, then, according to I Thessalonians 5:18, thank God in prayer for these things. Also, make a list of the areas of your life where you have failed to live responsibly and faithfully and then seek to do those things which God wants you to do, no matter how you feel. How are you failing as a husband/wife, mother/father, church member, employee, citizen? What abilities, talents, or opportunities are you overlooking or failing to use? Make a list of things you do have and think of them instead of what you don't have. Make a list of all the things you can and should do and then plan a schedule when you will do them and get busy. For the next week, keep a record of all the profitable things you do. When you are tempted to think wrongly, ask God for help to do His will, remind yourself of what Scripture says you should think and do and of all the profitable things you have on your lists. Then get busy thinking and doing these profitable things. As you consistently follow this procedure, God will help you to change your thought patterns (Rom. 12:1, 2; II Cor. 10:4, 5).

USEFULNESS

How to Become a Useful Person

A. Briefly write out your definition of a successful person.

_____

_____

In what two categories did God define the realm of Adam's usefulness in Genesis 1:28?

_____

In what specific ways did Adam fulfill these overall purposes?

Genesis 2:15: _____

Genesis 2:20: _____

Genesis 2:18: _____

According to Genesis 2:24, where was Adam and Eve's primary sphere of

service? _____

In the light of the above verses, how would you answer the following question: "Why should I be concerned about being a useful person?"

_____

_____

B. God created man as the crowning reflection of Himself; He created man in His own image. Because God is a God of order and purpose (and certainly the very fact that His creation was pronounced "good" indicates usefulness), He put man in the garden of Eden to be useful and productive. Man's labors brought glory to God. The most essential part of man's usefulness was that he was rightly related to God, and his works glorified God. But when Adam and Eve sinned against God, they demonstrated an unwillingness to serve God. They willingly and knowingly broke God's law to further their own selfish cause (Gen. 3:6). As the result of their sin they lost fellowship with God (Gen. 3:24), and the guilt of their sin was also charged to the account of all mankind. Life became a burden and a hardship from that time forth, not only for Adam and Eve but also for their posterity (Gen. 3:14-19). Because all of mankind is sinful and cannot by personal efforts merit God's favor or become

183

useful according to God's plan (Rom. 3:11), what does the Bible say must take place in a person's life before His efforts can ever please God and before he can be restored to God's original design?

Psalm 51:10-13: _____

John 3:3: _____

II Corinthians 5:17: _____

I Corinthians 2:9-16: _____

_____

John 15:5: _____

Titus 3:4-7: _____

Have you been born again by the Holy Spirit? As the result of the new birth have you trusted in Christ as the only Saviour from your sins and are you presently continuing to obey Him as Lord of your life?

_____

_____

Note: It is not possible to experience a prosperous, meaningful, and purposeful life and a life pleasing to God unless you have first of all received Jesus Christ as your Saviour and Lord and your life is being transformed by the power of the indwelling Holy Spirit. In fact, all efforts apart from a living relationship with Jesus Christ will only add to one's condemnation (Prov. 21:4; John 3:19; Col. 1:21).

C. According to Luke 12:15, what is often mistaken as an indication of true

success? _____

Consider the values of our present day society. Besides wealth and beauty, what are some other false and unbiblical standards of determining human worth and success?

Stardom   _____

_____   _____

_____   _____

_____   _____

D. According to the following verses, what must be foundational to have a truly prosperous, useful, and meaningful life?

Joshua 1:8: _____

Psalm 1:1-3: _____

Psalm 37:31: _____

Psalm 37:34: _____

Proverbs 15:16: _____

Matthew 7:24, 25: _____

John 13:17: _____

I Timothy 4:15: _____

Study Proverbs 6:13-18.

a. What does God value more than financial success?

_____

b. What is your definition of wisdom? _____

_____

c. List at least seven benefits derived from the daily application of the Scriptures mentioned in this passage.

_____	_____
_____	_____
_____	_____
_____	

Review your own life and check where you may be stressing unbiblical values and goals for yourself, family, and others.

E. According to the following verses, what will be the inevitable outcome of finding security and measuring success by means of popularity, financial success, status, beauty, etc., and the demise of those who are not in a right relationship with God through Jesus Christ and who refuse to abide by the Scriptures?

Psalm 1:4: _____

Psalm 37:35, 36: _____

Psalm 73:12, 18, 19: _____

_____

Ecclesiastes 5:10: _____

Proverbs 25:6, 7: _____

Isaiah 2:16-24: _____

Daniel 4:28-33: _____

Luke 12:16-21: _____

Luke 16:19-26: _____

F. Study the following verses to discover why God saves sinners.

John 15:8: _____

John 15:16: _____

Romans 8:29: _____

Ephesians 2:10: _____

Philippians 1:11: _____

Titus 2:14: _____

In your estimation, what should be the primary purpose for becoming a useful person?

_____

_____

G. Study the following verses to determine other Scriptural reasons for becoming a useful person.

Proverbs 31:27: _____

Matthew 25:14-46: _____

_____

John 15:11: _____

Romans 1:11: _____

Romans 16:1, 2: _____

I Corinthians 9:22: _____

Philippians 1:19-20: _____

I Peter 4:10: _____

I Timothy 1:16: _____

I Timothy 5:8: _____

H. Spiritual Gifts

1. What implications do the following verses have in connection with the

Christian's usefulness?

Ephesians 4:7: _____

Romans 12:3-6a: _____

_____

I Peter 4:11: _____

2. While referring to Romans 12:3, note why we should want to discover our spiritual gifts. _____

What is the function of spiritual gifts?

Romans 12:4, 5: _____

I Corinthians 12:7: _____

I Corinthians 12:25, 26: _____

I Corinthians 14:12: _____

Ephesians 4:11, 12: _____

I Peter 4:10: _____

3. Study I Corinthians 12:14-31. According to Paul, why is it necessary to have a diversity of spiritual gifts in the Body of Christ? (cf. vss. 17-19).

_____

What implications does the fact that every member of the Body of Christ has spiritual gifts of equal importance and unique ministry have upon the

Christian's usefulness? _____

_____

According to I Corinthians 12:13, 27 and Romans 12:4, 5, within what God-ordained framework will you be able to determine your spiritual gifts?

_____

Are you a member of a local church where the Bible is faithfully believed

and preached? _____

Are you seeking to have a fuller and deeper knowledge of Jesus Christ?

_____

How are you becoming better acquainted with the people in your church

so that you might become useful in their lives? _____

4. Using Romans 12:6-8; I Corinthians 12:8-10; I Corinthians 12:28; Ephesians 4:11, 12 as your guide, answer the following questions.

a. What things do you really like to do? _____

_____

_____

b. What are the things you do well? _____

_____

_____

c. From the items mentioned in the above two lists, what ministries did you perform that blessed and strengthened others? What have you done that has been favorably confirmed by others in the church?

_____

_____

Plan to discuss with your pastor your spiritual gifts. As you prepare to meet with him, make a list of what you consider to be your spiritual gifts. My spiritual gifts are (some may have been endowed with one gift, and others may have received more than one):

_____   _____

_____   _____

Ask your pastor where you may use your spiritual gifts to minister to your fullest potential (I Pet. 4:10).

I. Usefulness in the Church

Here are some verses that describe specific ways in which every Christian may become more useful in the ministry of the local church. Write down the various ministries Christians may perform in the church.

Romans 15:14: _____

Romans 1:8: _____

Romans 12:10, 11: _____

Romans 13:8: _____

Romans 14:13, 19: _____

I Corinthians 12:25: _____

Galatians 5:13: _____

Galatians 6:2: _____

Ephesians 4:1, 2: _____

Ephesians 4:32: _____

Ephesians 5:18-21: _____

II Corinthians 11:9: _____

II Corinthians 9:7: _____

Colossians 3:9, 12, 13, 16: _____
_____

I Thessalonians 3:12: _____

I Thessalonians 4:8: _____

I Thessalonians 5:11, 14: _____

Hebrews 10:23-25: _____

James 5:9, 16: _____

Hebrews 13:17: _____

Philippians 4:5: _____

I Peter 4:9: _____

I John 4:7, 11, 12: _____

II John 5: _____

J. Usefulness in the Home

   1. Look up the following verses and note some of the specific ways in which
      the husband may be useful in the home.

      Genesis 18:1-8: _____

      Deuteronomy 6:7: _____

      Proverbs 15:13: _____

      Proverbs 17:22: _____

      Proverbs 23:26: _____

      Proverbs 31:28: _____

Ephesians 5:23: _____

Ephesians 5:25: _____

Ephesians 5:28, 29: _____

Ephesians 6:4: _____

I Timothy 3:4, 5, 12: _____

I Timothy 5:8: _____

I Peter 3:7: _____

Deuteronomy 6:5: _____

In what areas can you as the husband become more useful in the home? In spending more time with your wife? with your children? Being more cheerful and fun to be with? Taking more of a lead in family worship? Becoming a better administrator?

Using the above verses as a guide (the list is by no means exhaustive) plan where and how you are going to make specific changes in becoming more useful in the home. Make it a point to implement these changes immediately.

My specific changes will be: _____

_____

_____

2. Look up the following verses and note some of the specific ways the wife may become useful in the home.

Genesis 2:18: _____

Proverbs 31:11, 12: _____

Proverbs 31:13: _____

Proverbs 31:15: _____

Proverbs 31:16: _____

Proverbs 31:21: _____

Proverbs 31:22: _____

Proverbs 31:24: _____

Proverbs 31:27: _____

Proverbs 14:1: _____

Ephesians 5:22, 33: _____

I Timothy 3:11: _____

Titus 2:4, 5: _____

I Peter 3:1: _____

I Peter 3:3, 4: _____

I Peter 3:5: _____

Are there areas in which you are failing as a wife/mother? Could you be more industrious at home? Could you be a more willing and affable companion to your husband? Write out how you will make some specific changes and become a more useful person in the home in order to please God and reverence your husband.

The specific changes I will make are: _____

_____

_____

Note: For a more definitive list of ways women may become more useful in the home, church, and community, refer to the study entitled "How a Christian Woman Can Become Useful" (p. 219).

3. What implications do the following verses have in connection with children's usefulness in the home?

Ephesians 6:1: _____

Ephesians 6:2: _____

Psalm 127:4, 5: _____

Psalm 128:3: _____

Proverbs 1:8: _____

Proverbs 3:21: _____

Proverbs 4:1: _____

Proverbs 10:1a: _____

Proverbs 10:5 _____

Titus 2:3, 4: _____

Proverbs 23:15, 16: _____

Proverbs 23:22: _____

Proverbs 23:23, 24: _____

Proverbs 29:11: _____

Proverbs 31:28: _____

Genesis 45:1-15: _____

Are there some specific areas where you as a child may become more useful in the home? List them. Are you endeavoring to faithfully do your daily chores? Are you willing to learn from your parents' instruction and put it into practice? Are you looking for opportunities to do more than what is required of you?

In the following spaces write down how you are failing and plan to change immediately by putting into action what you should be doing to become more useful.

My specific changes will be _____

_____

_____

K. Study the following verses and answer the questions as they relate to the continued *usefulness of the elderly and grandparents*.

1. Read Joshua 14:6-15. According to verse 6, how old was Caleb when he

   was commissioned by Moses to spy out the Land of Canaan? _____

   How old was he when Joshua allotted to him his portion of the conquered

   land? _____ Read verses 11 and 12. How did

   Caleb indicate a zealous, vigorous, and optimistic outlook on life?

   _____

   _____

2. Read Ruth 4:13-17. How did Naomi find usefulness as a grandmother?

   (cf. vs. 16) _____

3. What attitudes did the elderly Anna possess? (Luke 2:36-38) _____

   _____ In what specific ministry was she

   engaged? _____.

4. When Abraham and Sarah died, how would you describe their attitude

   toward life? (Heb. 11:13) _____

   _____

5. In what very important way did Timothy's grandmother influence him? (II Tim. 1:5) _____

6. How does each of these verses illustrate the importance and blessings of work?

   Genesis 2:15: _____

   Proverbs 14:23: _____

   Ecclesiastes 5:12: _____

   Revelation 7:13: _____

   Revelation 22:3: _____

   What implications do these verses have upon the retired Christian? Should

   retirement exclude all forms of work? _____

   _____

7. Rather than focus on what you cannot do, what does Romans 12:3 tell you

   to do? _____

   What character qualities and specific ministry should older Christian women

   have? (Tit. 2:3-5; I Tim. 5:11; Luke 2:36, 37) _____

   _____

   Make a list of some specific ways you as an elderly woman may have a more

   useful ministry in the home, church, and community. _____

   _____

   _____

   What implications does Titus 2:2 have in reference to an older Christian

   man's usefulness? _____

   _____

   _____

   How can you use your time, gifts, talents, skills, home, wisdom, etc., to

   serves Christ and others? _____

   _____

   _____

8. Study Psalm 92:12-14. Before an elderly person can be fruitful, what must take place in his life? (vs. 13) _____

_____

What does the Bible say will take place in an older person's life if he is willing to serve God and desires to continue to grow? (vs. 14) _____

_____

_____

Biblically speaking, should old age be a blessing or a burden? _____

Why? _____

How can you continue to grow spiritually?

_____

How can you continue to become a more interesting person? _____

_____

L. Usefulness in the World

In what specific way can you become useful in the world. Notice that some of the verses describe the attitudes with which you should perform your tasks.

Category 1

Titus 2:9, 10: _____

Colossians 3:22, 23: _____

Ephesians 6:6-8: _____

Matthew 5:41: _____

Ecclesiastes 5:12: _____

Proverbs 10:4; 21:5: _____

Proverbs 13:17: _____

Proverbs 25:13: _____

Luke 16:10: _____

I Peter 2:18-20: _____

In what specific ways can you become a more conciliatory, diligent, faithful, and helpful employer/employee? _____

_____

_____

Category 2

Luke 16:9: _____

Luke 5:41: _____

Galatians 6:10: _____

Ephesians 5:16: _____

Luke 10:30-37: _____

_____

Proverbs 18:14: _____

In what specific ways can you use your money, time, resources, opportunities to build relationships with other people in order to bring them to Christ?

_____

Category 3

I Peter 2:17: _____

Romans 13:1, 6, 7: _____

Titus 3:1: _____

I Timothy 2:1, 2: _____

Make a list of the specific ways you as a Christian can become a more conscientious and dedicated citizen. Example: "Determine to drive 55 mph in order to save gas." Example: "Pay your income taxes without complaining" (Phil. 2:14).

_____

_____

_____

Begin immediately to keep informed on the various issues involving our country and its leaders. Make a list of current issues that ought to concern Christians. Pray specifically for your country's leaders, the decisions they have to make, and the current affairs affecting the lives of our country's people.

How a Christian Woman Can Become Useful

The problem of judging themselves to be useless and worthless is a problem that many women in our day face. Their husbands are out in the world facing new and sometimes exciting situations each day, holding positions of responsibility and importance outside the home as well as inside the home, and contributing to the welfare of their companies as well as providing the physical necessities of their families. Many women who are not career-oriented and who are involved in the same apparently menial and unnoticed tasks week after week are easily tempted to judge themselves to be useless and worthless. Some react by taking upon themselves responsibilities which God intended for men only. This catalog of verses illustrates both by precept and by example the many areas in which a Christian woman may have a meaningful ministry. Check the references which challenge you to make some specific changes and implement them immediately in your life. Ask for the counsel of your husband, pastor, or trusted Christian friend as to how you may become a more effective servant of Jesus Christ. (It is the responsibility of every husband to encourage his wife to accomplish and contribute something which would be consistent with the Word of God—Eph. 5:28, 29.)

Usefulness in the Home

Genesis 18:6: _____

Genesis 24:67: _____

Ruth 1:6-8, 14-16: _____

Psalm 128:3: _____

Proverbs 1:8; 6:20: _____

Proverbs 31:11: _____

Proverbs 31:15, 21: _____

Proverbs 31:16, 24: _____

Proverbs 31:22: _____

Proverbs 31:27: _____

Ephesians 5:22, 33: _____

I Timothy 2:11: _____

I Timothy 5:14: _____

Titus 2:4, 5: _____

II Timothy 1:5: _____

Usefulness in the Church

Luke 2:26-28: _____

Luke 7:36-38: _____

Luke 10:39: _____

John 4:25: _____

Write out how you can become more effective in bringing other people to Christ. Plan how you will implement at least one of the suggestions.

Having women's coffee hour and Bible _____

study _____ _____

_____ _____

_____ _____

Study I Timothy 5:10. What specifications does Paul list as those describing an honorable widow and one who should receive the support of the church?

_____

_____

In what way is the Shunammite widow an example of one who "took in strangers"?

I Kings 4:8-11) _____

_____

How will you begin to minister more effectively in the area of hospitality?

Offer spare bedrooms to visiting families _____

_____

_____

_____

In what specific way was Abigail an example of "washing the feet of the saints" (cf. I Sam. 25:14-18, 32, 33, 41; see also Acts 9:36-39).

_____

_____

How could you begin to minister to those who are in need and to do those practical jobs around the church which are necessary and important but not necessarily noticed?

Offer to baby-sit _____

_____

_____

_____

How was Phoebe in Romans 16:1, 2 an example of "relieving the afflicted"?

_____

In what specific ways can you begin to relieve the burden of the afflicted?

Make clothes for a needy family _____

_____

_____

_____

Titus 2:3-5: _____

_____

How can you teach other women the truths of Christianity and how these truths relate to practical Christian living?

Share good Christian literature

Exchange recipes _____

Be an example of punctuality and orderliness _____

_____

_____

_____

_____

Usefulness in the World

Proverbs 31:16: _____

Proverbs 31:24: _____

Proverbs 31:23: _____

Acts 16:14: _____

In what specific ways can you become more useful in the world?

Volunteer to participate in child care _____

_____

_____

_____

Suggested Ministries and Services:

Typing and correspondence
Being a good listener
Involved in prayer chain
Teach others to sew, cook
Offer transportation
Visit the sick
Offer to cook, do laundry for sick person
Clean the church
Honor your parents
Help pastor by searching for sermon illustrations
Teach other women how to arrange flowers, etc.
Have a neighborhood children's Bible story club
Be your husband's companion

Cheerfulness
Counseling women
Teach women's Bible studies
Children's work
Prayer for others
Testifying and witnessing
Visitation
Wise purchaser
Be a good domestic engineer
Community projects
Ministry of music
Encourage and comfort
Lead or participate in women's clubs, projects, groups
Write Christian literature
Lead or work in DVBS

VOCATION

(Getting a Job, Career Selection)

1. List all the jobs you are capable of doing. List the jobs you have had and your reasons for leaving those jobs.
2. List the jobs you would like to have in order of preference. Get all the facts you can about these jobs by talking to people who have them or by reading literature about them. Check your local library for information about various occupations. Especially look for the Occupational Outlook Handbook or *The Dictionary of Occupational Titles.*
3. Visit your State Employment Office or the Human Resources Development Office and take an aptitude test. Ask about required training for jobs and placement service.
4. Check the job advertisements in newspapers and make calls for appointments.
5. Go through the yellow pages of the telephone directory and make a list of every company that may possibly use people with skills, abilities, and interests like yours. Also get a book with all of the industries and businesses in your area from your local chamber of commerce and write down the same information from this book. Once you have made your list, get on the telephone and call the various businesses and industries to see if any of them need your skills and abilities.
6. Talk to people in your church and community. Ask Christians to pray with you. Ask everyone to give you any suggestions they may have.
7. Talk to a number of people involved in the work in which you are interested. Find out everything you can about the job—the nature of the work, how to prepare, its problems, responsibilities, potential and benefits, how to get the job, the working conditions on the job, its influence on your personal, family, or spiritual life, how it fits into your desire to serve Christ.
8. Check the computer in a public library of a large city for jobs available in your area of interest.
9. Get a good book on how to write a resume. Read it and write a good resume. Have a Christian employer check it over and make suggestions.
10. Do the Bible study on "Guidance" by Wayne Mack and Raymond Richards.

WORK

Study the following verses and write down everything they have to say about work. Evaluate your own attitude and conduct in the light of what you discover. Write down specific ways in which you need to change. Keep a daily record for the next week of how many hours you work and what kinds of things you do.

Proverbs 6:6-9: _____

Proverbs 10:4, 5, 26: _____

Proverbs 12:11, 24, 27: _____

Proverbs 13:4: _____

Proverbs 14:23: _____

Proverbs 15:19, 27: _____

Proverbs 18:9: _____

Proverbs 19:15, 24: _____

Proverbs 20:4, 13: _____

Proverbs 21:25, 26, 29: _____

Proverbs 22:2, 13, 29: _____

Proverbs 24:30-34: _____

Proverbs 25:19: _____

Proverbs 26:13, 14, 15, 16: _____

Proverbs 27:23-27: _____

Proverbs 28:19, 20, 24: _____

Proverbs 31:10-31: _____

Ecclesiastes 5:12: _____

Ecclesiastes 9:10: _____

Ecclesiastes 10:18: _____

Ecclesiastes 11:4, 6: _____

Genesis 2:7, 15: _____

Exodus 20:8-11: _____

Exodus 23:12: _____

Exodus 35:2: _____

Deuteronomy 5:13: _____

I Kings 11:28: _____

Matthew 9:37, 38: _____

Matthew 20:1-9: _____

Acts 18:3: _____

Acts 20:33-35: _____

Romans 12:11: _____

Ephesians 4:28: _____

Ephesians 6:5-8: _____

Colossians 3:22-24: _____

I Thessalonians 4:10-12: _____

II Thessalonians 3:10, 11: _____

I Timothy 5:8, 13, 14: _____